An Analysis of

Martin Buber's

I and Thou

Simon Ravenscroft

Published by Macat International Ltd
24:13 Coda Centre, 189 Munster Road, London SW6 6AW.

Distributed exclusively by Routledge
2 Park Square, Milton Park, Abingdon, Oxon OX14 4RN
711 Third Avenue, New York, NY 10017, USA

Routledge is an imprint of the Taylor & Francis Group, an informa business

www.macat.com
info@macat.com

Cataloguing in Publication Data
A catalogue record for this book is available from the British Library.
Library of Congress Cataloguing-in-Publication Data is available upon request.
Cover illustration: Jonathan Edwards

ISBN 978-1-912453-79-5 (hardback)
ISBN 978-1-912453-61-0 (paperback)
ISBN 978-1-912453-67-2 (e-book)

Notice
The information in this book is designed to orientate readers of the work under analysis,
to elucidate and contextualise its key ideas and themes, and to aid in the development
of critical thinking skills. It is not meant to be used, nor should it be used, as a
substitute for original thinking or in place of original writing or research. References and
notes are provided for informational purposes and their presence does not constitute
endorsement of the information or opinions therein. This book is presented solely for
educational purposes. It is sold on the understanding that the publisher is not engaged
to provide any scholarly advice. The publisher has made every effort to ensure that
this book is accurate and up-to-date, but makes no warranties or representations with
regard to the completeness or reliability of the information it contains. The information
and the opinions provided herein are not guaranteed or warranted to produce particular
results and may not be suitable for students of every ability. The publisher shall not be
liable for any loss, damage or disruption arising from any errors or omissions, or from
the use of this book, including, but not limited to, special, incidental, consequential or
other damages caused, or alleged to have been caused, directly or indirectly, by the
information contained within.

CONTENTS

THE MACAT LIBRARY

The Macat Library is a series of unique academic explorations of seminal works in the humanities and social sciences – books and papers that have had a significant and widely recognised impact on their disciplines. It has been created to serve as much more than just a summary of what lies between the covers of a great book. It illuminates and explores the influences on, ideas of, and impact of that book. Our goal is to offer a learning resource that encourages critical thinking and fosters a better, deeper understanding of important ideas.

Each publication is divided into three Sections: Influences, Ideas, and Impact. Each Section has four Modules. These explore every important facet of the work, and the responses to it.

This Section-Module structure makes a Macat Library book easy to use, but it has another important feature. Because each Macat book is written to the same format, it is possible (and encouraged!) to cross-reference multiple Macat books along the same lines of inquiry or research. This allows the reader to open up interesting interdisciplinary pathways.

To further aid your reading, lists of glossary terms and people mentioned are included at the end of this book (these are indicated by an asterisk [*] throughout) – as well as a list of works cited.

Macat has worked with the University of Cambridge to identify the elements of critical thinking and understand the ways in which six different skills combine to enable effective thinking.
Three allow us to fully understand a problem; three more give us the tools to solve it. Together, these six skills make up the **PACIER** model of critical thinking. They are:

ANALYSIS – understanding how an argument is built
EVALUATION – exploring the strengths and weaknesses of an argument
INTERPRETATION – understanding issues of meaning

CREATIVE THINKING – coming up with new ideas and fresh connections
PROBLEM-SOLVING – producing strong solutions
REASONING – creating strong arguments

To find out more, visit **WWW.MACAT.COM.**

CRITICAL THINKING AND *I AND THOU*

Primary critical thinking skill: CREATIVE THINKING
Secondary critical thinking skill: PROBLEM-SOLVING

Martin Buber's *I and Thou* sets out to shed new light on what he considered an obscured dimension of human social life, what he called the "I-Thou relation." Over many drafts, he wrestled with the problem of finding the right terminology and means of expression for his message. His conundrum was as follows: how can you find a language to convey your message, when what you are trying to capture is ultimately beyond linguistic expression? After all, for Buber, the reality he had in mind was as much spiritual as it was philosophical. It was, for him, something that could only really be lived out, not something that could be contained in a text.

I and Thou is one of the key works of creative thinking in the Macat library, because Buber's response was to develop an entirely new way of thinking about human existence, divided between I-Thou and I-It modes.
He also expressed this new way of thinking in a novel and unusual way for a work of philosophy, using the language of imagination as much as the language of reason. Through both the form of expression and the content of his ideas, Buber manages to surprise the reader by introducing the element of the unexpected. He redefines the basic structure of human existence, enabling us to reflect on our lives from an entirely fresh perspective.

ABOUT THE AUTHOR OF THE ORIGINAL WORK

Born in Vienna, Austria in 1878, **Martin Buber** was a Jewish philosopher, widely regarded as the most influential Jewish intellectual of his generation. He worked across many different fields, but is best known for his philosophy of dialogue, first laid out in *I and Thou*, where he defines the human individual in terms of relationships. Buber's ideas in this area have had a wide influence across many academic disciplines from philosophy and theology to psychology, politics, and economics, as well as in the public sphere. He taught from 1938 at the Hebrew University in Jerusalem, retiring in 1951. In the latter part of his life he received numerous prestigious awards, including the Peace Prize of the German Book Trade, the Israel Prize in the humanities, and the Erasmus Prize. Buber died in Jerusalem in 1965 at the age of 87.

ABOUT THE AUTHOR OF THE ANALYSIS

Dr Simon Ravenscroft is a Research Associate at the Von Hügel Institute for Critical Catholic Inquiry at St Edmund's College in the University of Cambridge. His research interests run across the disciplines of theology, philosophy, social theory, and literature. His doctoral dissertation at Cambridge (2015) looked at the relationship between society and economy through an analysis of the work of the Catholic radical Ivan Illich.

ABOUT MACAT

GREAT WORKS FOR CRITICAL THINKING

Macat is focused on making the ideas of the world's great thinkers accessible and comprehensible to everybody, everywhere, in ways that promote the development of enhanced critical thinking skills.

It works with leading academics from the world's top universities to produce new analyses that focus on the ideas and the impact of the most influential works ever written across a wide variety of academic disciplines. Each of the works that sit at the heart of its growing library is an enduring example of great thinking. But by setting them in context – and looking at the influences that shaped their authors, as well as the responses they provoked – Macat encourages readers to look at these classics and game-changers with fresh eyes. Readers learn to think, engage and challenge their ideas, rather than simply accepting them.

'Macat offers an amazing first-of-its-kind tool for interdisciplinary learning and research. Its focus on works that transformed their disciplines and its rigorous approach, drawing on the world's leading experts and educational institutions, opens up a world-class education to anyone.'

Andreas Schleicher
Director for Education and Skills, Organisation for Economic
Co-operation and Development

'Macat is taking on some of the major challenges in university education ... They have drawn together a strong team of active academics who are producing teaching materials that are novel in the breadth of their approach.'

Prof Lord Broers,
former Vice-Chancellor of the University of Cambridge

'The Macat vision is exceptionally exciting. It focuses upon new modes of learning which analyse and explain seminal texts which have profoundly influenced world thinking and so social and economic development. It promotes the kind of critical thinking which is essential for any society and economy. This is the learning of the future.'

Rt Hon Charles Clarke, former UK Secretary of State for Education

'The Macat analyses provide immediate access to the critical conversation surrounding the books that have shaped their respective discipline, which will make them an invaluable resource to all of those, students and teachers, working in the field.'

Professor William Tronzo, University of California at San Diego

WAYS IN TO THE TEXT

KEY POINTS

- Martin Buber was a Jewish philosopher, most noted for his philosophy of dialogue.*

- *I and Thou* argues that human existence has two modes or attitudes, the "I-It" and the "I-Thou."

- With this, Buber proposes an entirely new way of thinking about human existence.

Who was Martin Buber?

Born in Vienna, Austria in 1878, Martin Buber is often regarded as the most influential Jewish intellectual of his generation. His work spanned many different fields, from philosophy to biblical studies to politics and psychology, but he is primarily known for the ideas set out in his book *I and Thou*, focusing on the principle of dialogue. His ideas were influenced by his Jewish heritage, but Buber was also well educated in the tradition of western philosophy, and it is this combination of perspectives that enabled him to speak powerfully to a wide audience during his lifetime. In the period after *I and Thou*, much of Buber's work sought to deepen the philosophy laid out in the book and apply it to new spheres, though he also embarked on quite different projects such as a substantial new translation of the Hebrew Bible into German.

Buber was the recipient of numerous prestigious awards in his lifetime, including the Peace Prize of the German Book Trade (1953), his acceptance of which—as a Jewish figure accepting a German award so soon after the Holocaust*—was itself a political statement; the Israel Prize, considered the highest honor given by the state of Israel, awarded for his contributions to the humanities (1958); and the Erasmus Prize (1963), recognizing the importance of his work in deepening the spiritual life of the people of Europe. He exerted a personal influence over a number of political leaders during his life, including Dag Hammarskjöld,* then the Secretary-General of the United Nations, who nominated Buber for the Nobel Peace Prize in 1959.[1] Buber died in 1965 at the age of 87.

What does *I and Thou* say?

In *I and Thou* (original German: *Ich und Du*), Martin Buber argued that humans engage with the world in two different ways. The first is that of an "I" towards an "It." This is where an individual stands apart from a particular object in order, for example, to use, manipulate, or classify it and so differentiate it from other objects. This way of engaging with the world is detached and impersonal. The "It" can also be another person, who is being treated more as an object or a number.

The other form of engagement is that of an "I" towards a "Thou" (or "You"). This "I-Thou" relation can exist between humans and nature or God, but it is easiest to understand as a relation between people. In this case, an individual would meet another human in a much more personal way, as a "Thou" or "You" rather than "He" or "She" or "It." This way of meeting others goes beyond thoughts of how that person might be useful, or how one might define or classify an individual from a distance. Instead it is about forming a relationship of wholeness or unity, but one that still accounts for the difference and uniqueness of the two parties.

Buber argued that both the I-It and the I-Thou ways of engaging with the world are important. The I-It attitude is necessary for co-ordinating human activity in the world, in order to produce the materials and institutions needed to sustain biological life, for example. But he believed that humans truly find meaning in relations of the I-Thou sort. Humans become most fully themselves only by forming this sort of personal connection with others, with nature, and ultimately with God. Part of Buber's aim in *I and Thou* was to warn his readers not to neglect the I-Thou, at a time when he felt modern society—with its increasing reliance on technology and industry, and faith in human power to manipulate nature—was in danger of becoming dominated by I-It attitudes.

I and Thou put forward an entirely new theory regarding the structure of human existence, and the vision at the heart of the book is simple but compelling. It argues that to be human is to form meaningful relationships, and that this interpersonal dimension of our existence is what matters most, ultimately bringing us into contact with God. While this is not in itself a complicated argument, its implications extend still to all spheres of human life, from the religious, to the political and economic, to the personal and the psychological.

The book was recognized as a groundbreaking contribution to philosophy and theology soon after its publication in German in 1923, and its subsequent translation into English in 1938. It forms the center-point of Buber's broader philosophy of dialogue, and its ideas have been explored and applied within an exceptionally wide range of disciplines. It is now rightly considered a classic of twentieth-century religious philosophy, not just in the West but globally, having been translated into at least 23 languages.[2]

Why does *I and Thou* matter?

I and Thou is a work that challenges its readers to reconsider their assumptions about how human life is structured, and about what gives it meaning. As with all true philosophy, the work encourages us to think critically about how to live, and about what makes a "good life." Should we place most value on those things and people that are useful to us? Or are there more important considerations than usefulness when thinking about what gives our lives meaning? These sorts of questions seem relatively simple, but they have very wide implications for how we arrange our lives and decide on our priorities.

I and Thou is also interesting for its writing style. Buber did not believe that the I-Thou relation was something that could ultimately be explained in technical language. Instead, he thought it was something that had to be lived out or acted upon if it was really to be known and understood. This posed a problem for his text, however: how can you try to express in language an idea that ultimately is beyond linguistic expression? Buber responded by writing in a style that was unconventional for a philosophical and academic text. Instead of engaging in dry, technical conversations with other authors, the book explores its ideas through a series of aphorisms,* ordered by theme and often using poetic language. Because of this, *I and Thou* is a book that appeals as much to the imagination as to reason.

Buber's style encourages his readers to consider the limits of what can be expressed in formal, academic language. They may even conclude that such a different form of presentation–at first sight unsuitable for an academic work–might actually be better for conveying some of our most important ideas. This non-technical style also makes this a good first text for readers who are coming to philosophy or theology from other disciplines. Buber's book is not written in a way that demands a lot of prior knowledge of philosophy or theology. The text is no less valuable for readers already familiar with those disciplines, however, because the questions it raises are so deep and fundamental that they will never be easily exhausted.

NOTES

1 See Maurice Friedman, *Encounter on the Narrow Ridge: A Life of Martin Buber* (New York: Paragon House, 1991), 409–19.

2 Avraham Shapira, *Hope For Our Time: Key Trends In The Thought of Martin Buber*, trans. Jeffrey M. Green (Albany, NY: State University of New York Press, 1999), 1.

SECTION 1
INFLUENCES

MODULE 1
THE AUTHOR AND THE
HISTORICAL CONTEXT

KEY POINTS

- *I and Thou* is a widely influential exploration of what it means to be human.
- Buber's text was influenced by both positive and negative relationships that he had in his life.
- Buber's experiences of World War I* led to a key turning point in his thinking.

Why Read This Text?

Martin Buber was arguably the most famous Jewish thinker of his generation, and among the most influential. While his various writings cross many disciplines, including philosophy, biblical studies, and social and political theory, his book *I and Thou*, first published in German in 1923, is his masterpiece, and contains his most important and influential ideas. The book proposed a new way of thinking about human existence in terms of two attitudes, the I-It and the I-Thou. It presents a vision of human life as finding its highest meaning in the principles of meeting, relation, and dialogue: in authentic encounters that we have with other humans, but also with nature, and through each of those finally with God (often referred to by Buber as the "eternal Thou").

This vision is relatively simple, but it has implications for all aspects of human life, including the religious, ethical, political, and psychological, each of which are explored in the book. Buber wrote his text in a creative, poetic and literary style, unconventional for a work of academic philosophy. This is because he believed the book's

> 66 All the areas of knowledge, experience, and thought to which he refers in his writings are decidedly marked with his personal stamp. The spiritual and ethical purpose is joined with the effort to reach a personal truth derived from life, from the special way in which a particular human life is lived. 99
>
> Avraham Shapira,* *Hope For Our Time: Key Trends in the Thought of Martin Buber*

central theme–the I–Thou relation–to be beyond technical, philosophical expression, as it referred to something that could only truly be lived out. *I and Thou* has had and continues to have influence across a broad range of disciplines, and is widely regarded as one of the most significant and original studies of the human condition in the twentieth century.

Author's Life

Martin Buber was born into a Jewish family in Vienna, Austria, in 1878. During his childhood his parents separated and he lived with his wealthy grandparents. His grandfather, Solomon Buber, was a respected scholar of rabbinic literature,* who helped to introduce Martin to Hasidic* and Zionist* thought. These proved to be lifelong interests. During his youth Buber also developed an interest in western philosophy, reading figures such as Immanuel Kant* and Friedrich Nietzsche.* He went on to study a variety of subjects including philosophy and psychology at universities in Vienna, Leipzig, Zurich, and Berlin, where he was taught by Wilhelm Dilthey* and Georg Simmel.*

Buber's mother left the family home when he was three years old and this difficult childhood experience had a lasting effect on him. He later coined the term "mismeeting" (German: *Vergegnung*) to describe his unsuccessful encounters with her.[1] Their impact on his philosophy is such that Buber's biographer has referred to them as the "decisive experience" of his life.[2] They influenced the writing of *I and Thou* serving for Buber as a stark contrast to the book's central theme of true meetings between people. Buber's happier relationships first with his grandparents and subsequently his wife Paula contributed more positively to the philosophical vision laid out in the book.[3]

Politically, Buber was involved with Zionism from a young age (he ultimately argued for the establishment of a bi-national state whereby land would be shared between Palestinians and Jews), and, before he wrote *I and Thou,* he published a range of texts on Hasidic themes. *I and Thou* marked a turning point, however, and his later work focused on developing the philosophy of dialogue expressed in its pages. He also undertook a substantial project translating the Hebrew Bible, initially with Franz Rosenzweig,* which he did not complete until 1961. Buber briefly held University positions in Frankfurt from 1923 until 1933, when he resigned in protest at the rise to power of the Fascist* Adolf Hitler.* In 1938 he left Germany to live in Jerusalem, where he taught at the Hebrew University until his retirement in 1951.

Author's Background

Buber spent his earliest childhood in Vienna and returned there to university as a young man around the turn of the twentieth century. Vienna during this period was known for its mood of artistic and intellectual creativity amidst the background decay of the old Hapsburg Empire.* This cultural atmosphere is often referred to by the French term *fin de siècle,* * and much of it, especially the Viennese theatre and styles of speaking and writing, seems to have had a profound effect on Buber. One commentator has remarked that "the spirit of Vienna in that era marked Buber's style for many years."[4] The strongly poetical and aphoristic style in which *I and Thou* is written, somewhat unusual for a philosophical text, shows this influence.

Buber began the first drafts of *I and Thou* while living in Germany during World War I, and completed it in the politically turbulent period immediately afterwards. Buber's own experiences and the general changing attitudes towards the War had a profound impact on his thought. Indeed, without them, *I and Thou* would not have taken the form it ultimately did. The war, Buber later commented, enabled him to see "the growing difficulty of genuine dialogue, and most especially of genuine dialogue between persons of different kinds and convictions."

"I began to understand at that time," he went on, "that this is the central question for the fate of mankind."[5] This led him to the realization that his earlier philosophy was inadequate because it lacked "the check of the faithful meeting with otherness" that would become a key subject of *I and Thou*.[6]

NOTES

1   Maurice Friedman, *Encounter on the Narrow Ridge: A Life of Martin Buber* (New York: Paragon House, 1991), 4-5; 131.

2   Friedman, *Encounter on the Narrow Ridge*, 4.

3   Friedman, *Encounter on the Narrow Ridge,* 5; 131-132.

4   Avraham Shapira, *Hope For Our Time: Key Trends In The Thought of Martin Buber*, trans. Jeffrey M. Green (Albany, NY: State University of New York Press, 1999), 13.

5   Martin Buber, "Hope for this Hour", in *Pointing The Way: Collected Essays of Martin* Buber, ed. Maurice Friedman, 222.

6   Friedman, *Encounter on the Narrow Ridge,* 85.

MODULE 2
ACADEMIC CONTEXT

KEY POINTS

- *I and Thou* draws on Jewish influences to address philosophical, religious, and social questions faced by western society.

- Thinkers like Nietzsche* and Marx* had set about a radical questioning of established philosophical, moral, political, and religious ideas.

- Buber was directly influenced by the Hasidic tradition, Kierkegaard,* Dilthey,* and Simmel,* among others.

The Work in its Context

I and Thou is a work of religious, specifically Jewish, philosophy but it was written by an author steeped in the traditions of western thought, and is set primarily in a western context. The book does not easily fit into any one discipline, since it fuses theological, philosophical, and socio-political themes in an unorthodox fashion. As one scholar has put it, Buber's work "crossed hitherto sacrosanct boundaries dividing scholarly disciplines."[1] The book ranges across so many disciplines, however, for the very reason that its main subject is so fundamental: the basic character of human interaction with others, with nature, and finally with God.

While *I and Thou* is indeed a work of Jewish thought, it should be understood in the context of a more general questioning of the received philosophical, religious, moral, social, and political ideas of the mid-to-late nineteenth and early twentieth centuries in western Europe. This questioning came from a variety of sources, and was a response not only to developments in thought, but also to the great

> 66 For all the fact that *I and Thou* is unthinkable without the wisdom of Hasidism and of the Hebrew Bible, in its form and its intent it is a universal book, concerned not with the Jews but with modern Western man. 99
>
> Maurice Friedman,* *Encounter on the Narrow Ridge*

material changes that western societies had undergone during the preceding century, as a result of scientific, technological, and industrial developments. It consisted often of dramatic rejections of dominant political, religious, or moral ideas, and radical new theories regarding the nature of human existence, from the structure of human societies to the structure of the human psyche.

Overview of the Field

Among the most influential of these radical questioners of the basic principles of western thought and society were three thinkers often referred to collectively as the Masters of Suspicion: Karl Marx, Friedrich Nietzsche, and Sigmund Freud.*[2]

Marx is famous primarily for his analysis and critique of the capitalist* economic system. He drew particular attention to the inhuman and degrading conditions of the working classes that had resulted from the mass industrialization* of the nineteenth century. Marx argued among other things that the course of human society in all its aspects, including religion, could be accurately explained by reference to material economic factors alone, such as the way goods are produced, traded, and consumed.

Nietzsche, for his part, had launched a powerful attack on Enlightenment* principles of morality and reason, as well as religious belief and practice. He interpreted human behavior and interactions—for example in the insistence upon moral norms—mostly in terms of people's desire for various kinds of power. He also spoke of the "death of God," foreseeing the end of traditional religion as well as of philosophical metaphysics.*

Finally, around the same time as Buber, Freud sought to explain human behavior in another new way, in terms of hidden psychological drives. Freud regarded religious beliefs, for instance, as "illusions, fulfilments of the oldest, strongest and most urgent wishes of mankind."[3] Freud pioneered the new field of psychoanalysis.* This combined a comprehensive theory of human psychology with a form of therapy to relieve its illnesses (or "pathologies"), while also offering a new lens through which to interpret human culture and society.

The work of these three thinkers illustrates the bold ways in which received ideas explaining human existence were being re-examined in the period just before Buber began his own career. It left open in a new way questions concerning the place of religion, and the role of ethics and morality in human life and society, as well as how one should explain and evaluate how humans act in relation to one another.[4]

Academic Influences

We can mention several significant direct influences on Buber, all of which he acknowledged in his lifetime. The first, emerging from Buber's Jewish upbringing, was his encounter with Hasidism. Buber drew on this tradition of mystical Judaism throughout his life, viewing it as a source of Jewish cultural renewal. Hasidic teachings emphasize the principles of presence and immediacy, as well as ineffability, or what Maurice Friedman has called "a meaning that can be lived and confirmed but cannot be defined."[5] Buber's notion of God, or the "Eternal Thou," as present to us in our encounters with other people is, moreover, consistent with his interpretation of the Hasidic emphasis on the immanence of God "not as an accomplished fact but as a task."[6]

Beyond Judaism, a further key long-term influence on the young Buber was the Christian existentialist* philosophy of Søren

Kierkegaard, most notably his stress on individuality, the uniqueness of any given situation, and the direct relation between the individual and God, addressed as "Thou."[7] Buber also seems to have identified with Kierkegaard's critique, as well as that of Fyodor Dostoevsky* and Nietzsche, of the mechanization of society and the emergence of mass culture. These he regarded as potentially harmful to the creation of meaningful personal relationships.[8]

Finally, while studying in Berlin, Buber attended talks by two key German thinkers on society, Wilhelm Dilthey and Georg Simmel. Both had a key influence on his thought in various ways. Dilthey, for example, made an important distinction between the different ways of approaching the sciences. The natural sciences (German: *Naturwissenschaften*) can be studied in a detached way. The human sciences (German: *Geisteswissenschaften*), on the other hand, require a more personal participation. Here, one sees a first glimmer of Buber's distinction between the "I-It" and "I-Thou" modes of engaging with the world.

Simmel's analysis of the interpersonal structure of human social life, and his emphasis on relation, were similarly important in the development of Buber's thinking.[9] A key area where Buber parts ways with Dilthey and Simmel concerns their account of "experience" (German: *Erlebnis*). For them, Buber later remarked, this "belonged to the exclusive, individualized, psychic sphere."[10] He, however, explicitly placed his idea of "meeting" well beyond this subjective sphere, warning that the encounters of which he spoke should not be "psychologized" into an "experience."[11]

NOTES

1   Paul Mendes-Flohr, Preface to *Martin Buber: A Contemporary Perspective*, ed. Paul Mendes-Flohr (Syracuse: Syracuse University Press and Jerusalem: The Israel Academy of Sciences and Humanities, 2002), vii.

2   Paul Ricoeur, *Freud and Philosophy: An Essay on Interpretation*, 2nd Edn, trans. Denis Savage (New Haven: Yale University Press, 2002), 33; 35.

3   Sigmund Freud, *The Future of an Illusion*, trans. W.D. Robson-Scott (London: Hogarth Press, 1953), 30.

4   Cf. Martin Buber, *Between Man and Man*, trans. Ronald Gregor Smith (London: Routledge and Kegan Paul, 1947), 137-156.

5   Maurice Friedman, *Encounter on the Narrow Ridge: A Life of Martin Buber* (New York: Paragon House, 1991), 52.

6   Friedman, *Encounter on the Narrow Ridge*, 68.

7   Maurice Friedman, *Martin Buber: The Life of Dialogue*, 4th edn. (London: Routledge, 2002), 39.

8   Friedman, *Encounter on the Narrow Ridge*, 47.

9   Paul Mendes-Flohr, *From Mysticism to Dialogue: Martin Buber's Transformation of German Social Thought* (Detroit: Wayne State University Press, 1989), 14; 25-30.

10 Martin Buber, "Replies to my Critics", in *The Philosophy of Martin Buber*, ed. Paul Arthur Schilpp and Maurice Friedman (LaSalle, IL: Open Court, 1967), 712; Mendes-Flohr, *From Mysticism to Dialogue*, 104-113.

11 Friedman, *Encounter on the Narrow Ridge,* 127.

MODULE 3
THE PROBLEM

KEY POINTS

- *I and Thou* explores the basic philosophical problem of what it means to be human.

- Important contributors to this debate include Kant, Feuerbach,* Marx, Nietzsche, and Heidegger.*

- Buber did not engage explicitly with these thinkers in *I and Thou*, but he did respond implicitly.

Core Question

Martin Buber's *I and Thou* addresses the basic question of what it means to be human in the world, which is to say the problem of philosophical anthropology.* In the book, Buber directly explores how humans relate to one another, to the wider world they inhabit, and to God or spirit.

Throughout the history of human thought, the questions "what is man?" and "how does the human relate to nature and to God," have been the subject of philosophical and religious enquiry. All the major religions and philosophical systems address them. With *I and Thou*, Buber is, therefore, contributing to an ancient and even timeless debate. His writing shows his broad education in the history of western philosophy and in the traditions of the Abrahamic faiths (especially, in his case, Hasidic Judaism). He would make his own personal journey on this question, too, later told in an essay in his book *Between Man and Man*. At fourteen, Buber writes, he became tortured by the thought of the infinity of space and time, and how to him both seemed "equally impossible, equally hopeless."[1] He briefly contemplated suicide, he says, until reading Immanuel Kant. The

> **&&** From time immemorial man has known that he is the subject most deserving of his own study, but he has also fought shy of treating this subject as a whole, that is, in accordance with its total character. **&&**
>
> Martin Buber, *Between Man and Man*

latter showed him that the problem he was wrestling with was not one of space and time as such, but the "mystery of [his] own comprehension of the world and the mystery of [his] own being."[2]

The Participants

This question—the mystery of what the human is—Buber sees as especially pressing in his own age. He describes his age as having a "special human homelessness and solitude," that has led to a "new setting of the anthropological question."[3] This was partly due to Kant, but also to others, such as Ludwig Feuerbach. Feuerbach is best known for his critique of Christianity. However, he also argued that "man's being is contained only in community, in the unity of man with man—a unity which rests, however, only on the reality of the difference between I and Thou."[4] This description of the human, balancing the uniqueness of the individual with an awareness of social situation, had a decisive influence on Buber.

Another important contributor to these discussions was Marx, whose response to the anthropological question was to describe the human in terms of material economic factors. Nietzsche also added to the argument in a distinctive way by presenting the human as a fundamentally "problematic being," who was always in the process of becoming, that is, of change.[5] The human differs from animals, in other words, because of a tendency to look toward the future. However, that orientation is defined by the pursuit of power, or what Nietzsche called "will to power." He describes his account of human psychology as "the doctrine of the development of the will to power."[6]

A final philosopher who is worth mentioning in this context is Martin Heidegger. He is relevant because at almost the same time as Buber, he too was asking fundamental questions about human beings. In his major work, *Being and Time*, published four years after *I and Thou* in 1927, Heidegger set about a re-examination of the question of Being. He did so, however, through an analysis of what he called *Dasein*,* a word which literally means "being-there" in German—the kind of being in the world that is peculiar to humans.[7] Although Heidegger went about his study in a different way to Buber, the fact that he was also addressing these themes around the same time reveals something of the general philosophical mood.

The Contemporary Debate

It is important to realize that Buber did not engage in *I and Thou* in an explicit debate with other thinkers. Instead, he writes in a literary style that develops its argument on its own terms. There is no question, however, that simply by putting forward an alternative picture of what it means to be human, Buber is responding implicitly to the work of others, including some of those mentioned above.

Helpfully, some of these connections are explored explicitly by Buber years later in *Between Man and Man*. Here Buber says that he disagrees with Marx, for example, because his emphasis on the role of material economic conditions in the progress of human society denies the human "power of decision."[8] And, while Buber admires Nietzsche for having "endow[ed] the anthropological question with unprecedented force and passion," he disagrees with him particularly on the idea that the chief human drive is what Nietzsche called "will to power."[9] "Greatness by nature includes a power," Buber says, "but not a will to power." The latter is rather the result of a kind of sickness.[10]

Buber's relationship to Heidegger is more complicated because the two were immediate contemporaries, though they did not engage in much direct dialogue. It is worth mentioning their respective attitudes to each other's work, as these were expressed slightly later, and this helps to highlight the fundamental differences between *I and Thou* and Heidegger's *Being and Time*. Heidegger is now known to have responded to Buber's concept of the I-Thou in lectures he gave in 1927 and 1928. Here, he implied that Buber had got ahead of himself: it was wrong of him to analyze the I-Thou as a mode of human existence, without a more fundamental examination of what existence means in general (something he saw himself providing through his exploration of Being as such in *Being and Time*).[11]

Buber does not seem to have known of this early response of Heidegger to his work. But Buber does engage with the ideas of *Being and Time* in his later book *Between Man and Man*. Here he argues that Heidegger's account of the human leaves no room for the interpersonal dimension of human existence: "Heidegger's self," he says, "is a *closed system*."[12] The emphasis of *I and Thou* on relationship is, as much as anything else, intended to combat this kind of picture of the human being as a *solitary* figure.

The way *I and Thou* is written, it is not necessary to know this wider philosophical context to understand the book, but doing so does enhance one's appreciation of the significance and novelty of what Buber achieved.

NOTES

1   Martin Buber, *Between Man and Man*, trans. Ronald Gregor Smith (London: Routledge and Kegan Paul, 1947), 136.

2   Buber, *Between Man and Man*, 137.

3   Buber, *Between Man and Man*, 134.

4   As quoted in Buber, *Between Man and Man*, 148.

5   Buber, *Between Man and Man*, 148.

6   Friedrich Nietzsche, "Beyond Good and Evil", in *Basic Writings of Nietzsche*, trans. and ed. Walter Kaufman (New York: Modern Library, 2000), 221 (§23).

7   Martin Heidegger, *Being and Time*, trans. John Macquarrie and Edward Robinson (Oxford: Blackwell, 1962).

8   Buber, *Between Man and Man,* 143-145.

9   Buber, *Between Man and Man*, 148.

10   Buber, *Between Man and Man*, 150-151.

11   Haim Gordon, *The Heidegger-Buber Controversy: The Status of the I–Thou* (Westport, CN: Greenwood, 2001), ix.

12   Buber, *Between Man and Man*, 171.

MODULE 4
THE AUTHOR'S CONTRIBUTION

KEY POINTS

- Buber's division of human existence into "I-Thou" and "I-It" attitudes was new and inventive.

- *I and Thou* was written in a literary style unusual for philosophy, but for important reasons.

- Buber's philosophy of dialogue was highly original, but also part of a broader philosophical trend.

Author's Aims

I and Thou addresses fundamental and perennial questions regarding the nature of human involvement in the world and in relation to God. However, Buber's way of answering these questions is highly inventive. His division of human existence into two distinct attitudes, that of the I-It and the I-Thou, is an original theory. Later in his career, Buber spoke in almost mystical terms about what inspired him, remarking that he felt "impelled by an inward necessity," and that a vision which he had had since his youth had come to a point of steady clarity and that he "had to bear witness to it."[1] For him, "A neglected, obscured primal reality was to be made visible," one that was–at the time– "barely paid attention to."[2] Among other things, his theory challenged prevailing scientific or technological modes of engagement with the world simply as something to be used. It also contested the terms of contemporary politics, and the rejection of faith in God, and re-emphasized the deep relational dimension of human life.

Buber's mode of presentation was also bold and inventive, and somewhat unorthodox for a philosophical text. *I and Thou* does not take the form of a logical argument, involving direct debate with other

> **" *I and Thou* has the structure of a symphonic composition. "**
>
> Paul Mendes-Flohr,* "Buber's Rhetoric"

authors. Rather, it is made up of a series of aphorisms arranged non-systematically and written in a highly poetical style. In *I and Thou*, "allusions and suggestive images are enjoined rather than carefully developed arguments."[3] This was, however, an approach Buber chose deliberately as the best way of conveying his message.

Approach

I and Thou was initially intended to be part of a much larger, five-volume systematic work, but Buber abandoned this plan on the basis that it would not serve as the right vehicle for his message. "No system was suitable for what I had to say," he would later remark.[4] Instead, he wrote *I and Thou* in a style that brings it closer to a work of literature than of traditional philosophy. As one scholar has put it, "I and Thou is more liked an extended prose-poem than a philosophical investigation." Yet, as he goes on, "This is intentional, of course; what Buber has to say demands a kind of poetry."[5]

The inventive and unusual way in which *I and Thou* was written should be understood as part of Buber's attempt to witness to the idea that the "I-Thou" relation–the main subject of the book–is always beyond full philosophical and discursive explanation. Buber is not attempting to explain exhaustively what the I-Thou relation is as a concept; he is even less interested in engaging in a tit-for-tat debate with other academics. Instead, he tries to point poetically towards a dimension of human existence–the depth of our relationships with others when they are authentic–that, according to him, can only be lived. For Buber, abstract philosophical systems were by nature too "monologic" (which means too "one-voiced") to convey an idea so tied to themes of dialogue, meeting, and relation. In this way, the literary form of *I and Thou* harmonizes with and reinforces its direct claims.

Contribution in Context

I and Thou is often referred to as the first full expression of Buber's "philosophy of dialogue," because of the emphasis it places on the relation between the self and the other. There were, however, a number of thinkers, Jewish and Christian, who around the same time, and largely independently of one another, came to develop similar philosophical and theological insights based on this principle of dialogue. They included Ferdinand Ebner,* Franz Rosenzweig, and Gabriel Marcel.*

Marcel wrote after Buber and so cannot have influenced him, but there is some question over the extent of Ebner and Rosenzweig's influence. Buber himself emphasized that he came to his conclusions independently of the work of these two thinkers, as well as that of another Jewish philosopher, Hermann Cohen.*[6] However, Rivka Horwitz* has shown that in the period in which he was drafting *I and Thou*, Buber read fragments of Ebner's work that would later be incorporated into Ebner's book, *The Word and the Spiritual Realities* (1921). Horwitz argues that Buber's exposure to this material contributed to his realization, expressed in *I and Thou*, that God can only be addressed as a "Thou," and cannot become an "It."[7]

During this period when he was drafting the book, Buber was engaged in direct dialogue with Rosenzweig. Although Buber did not read Rosenzweig's book *The Star of Redemption* (1921) until some time later, Rosenzweig's influence can, according to Horwitz, be seen in the way dialogue emerged as an explicit theme in Buber's thought around this period.[8] Dialogue had already been implicit in his work, but in the final drafts of *I and Thou* it took over from his earlier emphasis on ideas of "realization" and "orientation."

I and Thou is a deeply original work in both its form and content. It should also be regarded, though, as part of a broader trend among a small number of early twentieth century thinkers to put forward a philosophy based on an overarching principle of dialogue.

NOTES

1   Martin Buber, 1957 Postscript to *I and Thou*, trans. Ronald Gregor-Smith, 2nd edn. (Edinburgh: T&T Clark, 1958), 155.

2   Martin Buber, "Replies to my Critics", in *The Philosophy of Martin Buber*, ed. Paul Arthur Schilpp and Maurice Friedman (LaSalle, IL: Open Court, 1967), 692–3.

3   Paul Mendes-Flohr, "Buber's Rhetoric", in *Martin Buber: A Contemporary Perspective*, ed. Paul Mendes-Flohr (Syracuse: Syracuse University Press and Jerusalem: The Israel Academy of Sciences and Humanities, 2002), 23.

4   Buber, "Replies to my Critics," 693.

5   Roger Grainger, *Theatre and Relationship in Shakespeare's Later Plays* (Oxford: Peter Lang, 2008), 32.

6   Friedman, *Encounter on the Narrow Ridge,* 128.

7   Rivka Horwitz, *Buber's Way to "I and Thou": The Development of Martin Buber's Thought and His "Religion as Presence" Lectures* (New York, NY: Jewish Publication Society, 1988), 166-182.

8   Horwitz, *Buber's Way to I and Thou*, 214-239.

SECTION 2
IDEAS

MAIN IDEAS

KEY POINTS

- *I and Thou*'s main theme is the dual way in which humans engage with the world.

- Buber emphasizes the importance of being open to deep, authentic relationships with others, beyond thoughts of "use."

- The book's form, language, and style are unusual, but align with Buber's overall aims.

Key Themes

The primary theme of Martin Buber's *I and Thou* is what he calls the "twofold" attitude that humans bring to the world around them. By this he means that humans always relate to the world in one of two ways. One he designates with the term "I-It," and the other with the term "I-Thou."

The term I-It describes the detached attitude of the individual toward items of experience and use (with "experience" defined in a specific way by Buber, as explained in Module 2).[1] This is a mode of engagement where the self stands separate and apart from the object of perception, relating to the world and its contents as an "I" to an "It." This is a world in which things are objectified and bounded. They can be classified, measured, and manipulated (as in the manner of modern scientific methods, for example). The subject in the I-It attitude perceives the world as "ordered and detached" and is defined as an "individual" differentiated from other individuals.[2] The words "He" or "She" can be substituted for "It" insofar as it is possible to treat humans in this way as objects.

> ❝ To man the world is twofold, in accordance with his twofold attitude.
> The attitude of man is twofold, in accordance with the twofold nature of the primary words which he speaks...
> The one primary word is the combination *I-Thou*,
> The other primary word is the combination *I-It*;
> wherein...one of the words *He* and *She* can replace *It*. ❞
>
> Martin Buber, *I and Thou*

By contrast, the I-Thou attitude speaks to the relation that is created *between* (German: *zwischen*) the self and another, when the world and its contents are addressed personally as "Thou" (or "You"). This relation can come into being between people, and also between people and nature (he uses the example of a tree), and between people and "the eternal Thou," by which Buber means God or spirit. It is characterized by wholeness, or by the self and the other becoming bound up together in a unity. This unity nevertheless retains the uniqueness and difference of the two who meet in this way. In other words, the relationship is always dialogical. Unlike the I-It, the meeting of I and Thou is beyond measurement and classification. When the other is addressed as Thou, "he is not a thing among things, and does not consist of things."[3] The human comes to be a full self, a person, by entering into I-Thou relation.

Exploring the Ideas

For Buber, these categories were a way of explaining something very basic about the human condition: there is an impersonal world to be *used*, but also a personal world to be *met*. His book is not, however, a call to make a choice between the two. As Maurice Friedman has put it, "It has always been a complete misunderstanding of the I-Thou relationship to imagine that Buber thought it was possible or desirable to have only the I–Thou, or that he saw the I–It as evil in any way."[4] The I–It attitude is entirely necessary for material survival and for day-to-day human life. What Buber did see as evil, however, was "the refusal to return to the Thou,"[5] by confining oneself within the impersonal world of the "It." As he says, "without *It* man cannot live; but he who lives with *It* alone is not a man."[6]

A key part of Buber's argument is that the I–It attitude can come to eclipse the I–Thou attitude. On the individual level, Buber even says that this is inevitable, since any personal relationship must eventually become permeated with thoughts of usefulness and classification: "Now I may take out from him again the colour of his hair or of his speech or of his goodness."[7] That "every *Thou* in our world must become an *It*," Buber says, is "the exalted melancholy of our fate."[8] It means that humans spend their mortal lives swinging by nature "between *Thou* and *It*."[9]

On a more general level, however, the possibility of the I–It eclipsing the I–Thou is the greater danger for humankind, since it is to risk becoming lost in "nothingness."[10] Buber argues that relation, not separation or isolation, is fundamental for humanity ("In the beginning is relation") and that, "All real living is meeting."[11] In this sense, you are brought into the fullness of your existence and become truly yourself only through the I–Thou relation. For this reason, a key aim of Buber's text is to emphasize afresh for the western society of his day the "obscured primal reality" of the I–Thou relation,[12] at a time when Buber felt it was indeed in danger of being eclipsed by more detached, instrumental ways of thinking and acting. Buber describes this latter condition as a "sickness," and an "oppressive, stifling fate."[13]

Language and Expression

I and Thou is divided into three parts and is made up of a series of aphorisms of varying lengths. These are thematically organized but do not make up a strictly argued case. The first part introduces the distinction between the I–Thou and the I–It (terms that are, we should note, original to Buber) on the level of personal psychology. The second expands this primarily in the direction of society and public life, and the third more fully in the direction of religion. This aphoristic structure makes the work somewhat unsystematic, and its style is often strongly poetical and literary. Buber's approach depends more on the gradual elaboration of his central theme through thematic repetition than on the building of a logical case through rigorous analytical reasoning.

All this can make *I and Thou* seem slightly obscure or difficult to understand. Avraham Shapira is right to say that, "It is often difficult to follow the paths of Buber's thought, to get to the bottom of his ideas."[14] As discussed in Module 4, however, Buber made a deliberate decision to give the book this form. He did not believe that the I–Thou relation could be grasped by technical language, or that it was something for which one could provide a logical proof. Indeed, to try to explain it as if it were would, on Buber's terms, be to reduce it to the status of the "It," something that can be used or quantified or ordered, as if by a detached observer.

For Buber, in fact, the I–Thou relation is something that can only truly be lived. Thus, the aim of his text was to bear witness to this dimension of existence in a way that could fire the imagination as much as appeal to reason. Once this is appreciated, the book's fragmented, enigmatic, suggestive mode of presentation can be seen to be part of a cohesive vision, with the work's form and style in harmony with its philosophical content and ethical aims.

NOTES

1 Martin Buber, *I and Thou*, trans. Ronald Gregor-Smith, 2nd edn (Edinburgh: T&T Clark, 1958), 18.

2 Buber, *I and Thou*, 48; 85.

3 Buber, *I and Thou*, 21.

4   Friedman, "Martin Buber's Narrow Ridge", in *Martin Buber and the Human Sciences*, ed. Maurice Friedman (Albany, NY: State University of New York Press, 1996), 5.

5   Friedman, "Martin Buber's Narrow Ridge", 5.

6   Buber, *I and Thou*, 52.

7   Buber, *I and Thou*, 31.

8   Buber, *I and Thou*, 31.

9   Buber, *I and Thou*, 73.

10 Martin Buber, *I and Thou*, trans. Ronald Gregor-Smith, 2nd edn (Edinburgh: T&T Clark, 1958), 49.

11 Buber, *I and Thou*, 32; 25.

12 Martin Buber, "Replies to my Critics", in *The Philosophy of Martin Buber*, ed. Paul Arthur Schilpp and Maurice Friedman (LaSalle, IL: Open Court, 1967), 692–3.

13 Buber, *I and Thou*, 74-75.

14 Avraham Shapira, *Hope For Our Time: Key Trends In The Thought of Martin Buber*, trans. Jeffrey M. Green (Albany, NY: State University of New York Press, 1999), 13.

MODULE 6
SECONDARY IDEAS

KEY POINTS

- Buber acknowledges a place for economics and politics so long as they support genuine community.
- For Buber, we meet God in and through the I-Thou relations we forge with others.
- No significant ideas found in *I and Thou* have been overlooked by scholars.

Other Ideas

The central distinction in *I and Thou* is between the I-It and I-Thou ways of engaging with the world. In parts two and three of the book respectively, he applies this notion to questions of communal life (politics and economics) and religious faith. With regard to the former, Buber does not argue for an outright rejection of economics, which he defines as "will to profit," or the political State, which he defines in terms of the "will to be powerful."[1] Rather, he says that these spheres can and must be orientated toward, rather than away from, deeper participation in the spirit of the I-Thou relation.[2] As Buber puts it, "Economics…and the State…share in life as long as they share in [this] spirit." However, their effect is detrimental when they fail to do so:"If they abjure spirit they abjure life" (abjure means to renounce or reject).[3]

For Buber there is also a vital connection between the I-Thou and God, often referred to in the book as the "eternal Thou." For those who reject the term "God" altogether, Buber offers an account of God as One who can only ever be addressed as "Thou" and can never become an "It." That is to say, this One can never become an *object*, to

> 66 Men do not find God if they stay in the world. They do not find Him if they leave the world. He who goes out with his whole being to meet his *Thou* and carries to it all being that is in the world, finds Him who cannot be sought... If you hallow this life you meet the living God. 99
>
> Martin Buber, *I and Thou*

be treated or spoken about like any other object in the world.[4] Moreover, God is primarily encountered *through* the I-Thou relations that we establish in the world and not apart from them. Buber therefore says that "in each *Thou* we address the eternal *Thou*"[5] and that the eternal Thou is always already present in every other Thou: "Every particular *Thou* is a glimpse through to the eternal *Thou*."[6]

Exploring the Ideas

The substance of Buber's attitude to politics and economics is that these spheres of human activity can either serve the interests of genuine community or hinder them. This depends on where politics and economics, sectors ordinarily concerned with I-It attitudes, stand with respect to the I-Thou. Buber is clear that humans cannot in their communal life, any more than in their individual lives, "dispense with the world of *It*."[7] So, politics and economics cannot simply be rejected as a whole.

Rather, in order for these spheres to function in a healthy way, they must address a higher goal: "Man's will to profit and to be powerful have their natural and proper effect so long as they are linked with, and upheld by, his will to enter into relation."[8] Here, Buber is criticizing the idea that the spiritual dimension of life (the I-Thou) should be restricted to its own private and personal sphere, separate from politics, economics, and public life. He argues instead that the spirit of the I-Thou must be "reassimilated" into human communal life, since the "structures of man's communal life draw their living quality from the riches of the power to enter into relation."[9]

Buber's approach to the religious dimension in *I and Thou* centers on the principle of "mediation." This is the idea that God, or the "eternal Thou," is met in and through our meeting with any "Thou" in the world. In other words, for Buber, God's presence is *mediated* to us in the world "by means of every particular *Thou.*"[10] As with other parts of *I and Thou*, this is not meant as an abstract idea, but something to be lived out. Friedman is therefore right to say that, "Strictly speaking, Martin Buber has no philosophy of religion. What he says of Hasidism is true of his 'philosophy of dialogue': it does not wish to instruct us about God's nature but to show us the road on which we can meet God."[11]

The problem with many forms of religious speech, Buber argues, is that they have gradually come to refer to God not as a *Thou* but as an *It*; that is, in an impersonal and detached way, as if God were just a thing like other things. Buber thinks this is why, in the modern age, many people reject the word "God" completely, "because it is so misused."[12] Speaking of God and the world as entirely separate, or indeed speaking of them as entirely the same (as in pantheism*), are both the "language of *It*" according to Buber.[13] The task is to surpass these false alternatives, and instead to include "nothing beside God but everything in him."[14]

We saw in the last module how Buber claims that every particular "Thou" that we encounter in the world is destined to become, eventually, an "It." The importance of the spiritual dimension in Buber's book lies in his insistence that God is the only Thou for whom this will never be the case: "Only one *Thou* never ceases by its nature to be *Thou* for us."[15] Where God is met, in other words, it can only ever be in a real, present relation: "God is that being that is directly, most nearly, and lastingly, over against us, that may properly only be addressed, not expressed."[16]

Overlooked

Very few aspects of Martin Buber's *I and Thou* have been overlooked by scholars. Buber himself spent much of his own later career clarifying and developing the fundamental ideas in his short, concise text. Moreover, due to its significance, the work's various themes have also been explored from a wide range of perspectives in the secondary literature and few, if any, have have been neglected.

However, there are always new possibilities. Interesting work has recently been done, for example, within theological and religious studies on the importance of the doctrine of *creatio ex nihilo** as a common theme across the Abrahamic faiths (Christianity, Judaism, Islam). These investigations have significant implications for an understanding of the kind of relation that exists between God and the created order. This includes both the idea that God cannot be regarded as a "thing among things" and also the idea that God is present in and through created things.[17]

As we saw above, Buber discusses both of these points: that God is the eternal Thou who cannot be reduced to an "It" and that His presence is encountered in and through each particular Thou met in the world. Bringing Buber into this existing conversation could be a fruitful enterprise. Introducing his unique perspective would enrich it further, and also perhaps shed new light on the theological foundations of Buber's own account of the relation between God and the world.

NOTES

1   Martin Buber, *I and Thou*, trans. Ronald Gregor-Smith, 2nd edn (Edinburgh: T&T Clark, 1958), 69.

2   Buber, *I and Thou*, 62-70.

3   Buber, *I and Thou*, 49.

4   Buber, *I and Thou*, 99-100.

5   Buber, *I and Thou*, 19.

6   Buber, *I and Thou*, 99.

7   Buber, *I and Thou*, 68.

8   Buber, *I and Thou*, 68.

9   Buber, *I and Thou*, 69-71.

10 Buber, *I and Thou*, 99.

11 Maurice Friedman, *Martin Buber and the Eternal* (New York: Human Sciences Press, 1986), 15.

12 Buber, *I and Thou*, 99.

13 Buber, *I and Thou*, 103.

14 Buber, *I and Thou*, 104.

15 Buber, *I and Thou*, 127.

16 Buber, *I and Thou*, 106.

17 David B. Burrell *et al.,* eds. *Creation and the God of Abraham* (Cambridge: Cambridge University Press, 2010).

ACHIEVEMENT

KEY POINTS

- One can debate whether Buber's form of expression in *I and Thou* strengthens or weakens its achievement.

- *I and Thou*'s unique character is linked in important ways to its original circumstances.

- The book addresses universal problems in a general manner and is therefore not limited by these circumstances..

Assessing the Argument

Buber's inventive division of human existence into two modes, the I-It and the I-Thou, is clearly framed within *I and Thou* from the very first page. Most of the book is concerned with Buber's elaboration on this division and the various ways it applies to different spheres of human life, such as the political or the religious. As mentioned in previous modules, however, Buber made a conscious decision while drafting the book to avoid a systematic presentation. Instead the text is broken down into short aphorisms, and written in style somewhere between prose and poetry. As a result, Buber does not directly reference or converse with other philosophers or scholars in the book, in the way one would expect of a more conventional academic work.

This is both a strength and a weakness. On the one hand, the work's literary beauty and openness to interpretation is one reason for its influence across a wide audience (much wider than you might expect for a more technical work of philosophy). However, there is an inevitable loss of precision, making Buber's meaning more ambiguous than if he had chosen a more formal style. On the question of Buber's

> ❝ I have no teaching. I only point to something. I point
> to reality, I point to something in reality that had not or
> had too little been seen. I take him who listens to me
> by the hand and lead him to the window. I open the
> window and point to what is outside. ❞
>
> Martin Buber, "Replies to my Critics"

poetic language, Avraham Shapira has commented that, "Sometimes his linguistic artistry serves him faithfully. But sometimes he is captured by the charms of his own linguistic ability."[1] Walter Kaufman* has put it more bluntly, remarking that the book suffers from "suggestive but extremely unclear language."[2]

Kaufman's comment in particular seems to miss Buber's point that this mode of presentation was the only one suitable for his message. As Mendes-Flohr has put it, "Buber remained convinced that the word is not only a concept; it is an invocation of a primal reality that pulsates at the threshold of speech."[3] The literary form of the work is in that sense tied up with its core ideas. Buber could not simply, as Kaufman's remark seems to imply, have translated those ideas into a clearer idiom without losing some of his meaning.

Interestingly, while Buber often did go back and revise other of his writings, he chose never to do so with *I and Thou*, explaining his decision as follows: "At that time I wrote what I wrote in an overpowering enthusiasm. And what such inspirations deliver to one, one may no longer change, not even for the sake of exactness. For one can only measure what one might acquire, not what is lost."[4]

Achievement in Context

Martin Buber was himself quite candid about the influence of the historical context on *I and Thou*. He drew particular attention to the fact that the work was formulated and written during and shortly after the period of World War I. Against this background, he said, he "stood under the duty to insert the framework of the decisive experiences that I had at that time into the human inheritance of thought."[5] The duty that fell upon him, he felt, was to draw special and renewed attention to the I-Thou relation, because that was what his society needed at that time.

When he was later criticized for not giving due attention to the I-It attitude, his response was to draw attention to this historical context: "I am born in the midst of the situation of man and see what I see and must point out what I have seen. In another hour it would perhaps have been granted to me to sound the praises of the It; today not, because without a turning of man to his Thou no turn in his destiny can come."[6] When evaluating the achievement of *I and Thou*, therefore, it is important to consider that Buber chose his emphasis in response to the problems of his age. Writing at a different time, this emphasis might have been different. Thus, while the book has had long term influence across many contexts, the unusual character of *I and Thou* as a work of philosophy, and the uniqueness of its contribution, are closely related to the book's original historical setting.

That Buber wrote in a way that spoke to the needs of his time is borne out by the immediate success of the book in German. Gordon remarks that "*I and Thou* was soon accepted as a major contribution to philosophy and theology."[7] By 1930, some scholars had even suggested that the book would initiate a second Copernican Revolution* in philosophy.[8] While this can be seen in hindsight to have been an exaggeration, it conveys a sense of the extent of the initial enthusiasm for Buber's book. Slightly later, Emil Brunner* referred to Buber's description of the twofold attitude as "a profoundly revolutionary fundamental insight."[9] This gives a fair sense of Buber's achievement, as it was recognized in the immediate period after publication, and indeed in the longer term.

Limitations

While *I and Thou* was written in very particular historical circumstances–and while Buber himself drew attention to the individual nature of its message–in its broader impact the book has certainly transcended its original context. This is, in part, due to the open and general way in which the work was written. Buber was writing out of his own experiences in the context of European society in the post-World War I period, but he does not explicitly refer to either of these in the book. Rather, he sought, as he later put it, "to relate the unique and particular to the 'general', to what is discoverable by everyman in his own existence."[10]

This "general" scope explains the book's continuing appeal beyond its immediate academic fields of philosophy and theology. In addressing fundamental human questions, *I and Thou* "crossed hitherto sacrosanct boundaries dividing scholarly disciplines." But it did so meaningfully.[11] The same is true of the book's appeal beyond Buber's own Jewish religious tradition. In its pages, *I and Thou* speaks universally to the human race, and its audience has therefore been in no way limited to the members of a specific community or tradition.

Nevertheless, the work has sometimes provoked criticism from members of different religious traditions, particularly Christian and Jewish. For example, from a Jewish perspective, Eliezer Berkovits* criticized Buber for not being sufficiently faithful to the Jewish tradition, and for being too indebted to what he regards as Christian influences.[12] At the same time, and somewhat ironically, the Catholic theologian Hans Urs von Balthasar* criticized Buber for his work being insufficiently Christian and too Jewish in rejecting the divinity of Jesus Christ.[13] Other than this, however, the text has not been criticized notably in any more specific ways.

NOTES

1   Avraham Shapira, *Hope For Our Time: Key Trends In The Thought of Martin Buber*, trans. Jeffrey M. Green (Albany, NY: State University of New York Press, 1999), 15.

2   Walter Kaufman, "I and You: A Prologue," in Martin Buber, *I and Thou*, trans. Walter Kaufman (Edinburgh: T&T Clark, 1970), 24.

3   Paul Mendes-Flohr, "Buber's Rhetoric", in *Martin Buber: A Contemporary Perspective*, ed. Paul Mendes-Flohr (Syracuse: Syracuse University Press and Jerusalem: The Israel Academy of Sciences and Humanities, 2002), 23.

4   Martin Buber, "Replies to my Critics", in *The Philosophy of Martin Buber*, ed. Paul Arthur Schilpp and Maurice Friedman (LaSalle, IL: Open Court, 1967), 706.

5   Buber, "Replies to my Critics', 689.

6   Buber, "Replies to my Critics", 704.

7   Haim Gordon, *The Heidegger-Buber Controversy: The Status of the I–Thou* (Westport, CN: Greenwood, 2001), 115.

8   Robert E. Wood, *Martin Buber's Ontology: An Analysis of I and Thou* (Evanston: Northwestern University Press, 1969), XI-XII.

9   Emil Brunner, "Judaism and Christianity in Buber", in *The Philosophy of Martin Buber*, eds. Paul Arthur Schilpp and Maurice Friedman (LaSalle, IL: Open Court, 1967), 309-10.

10 Buber, "Replies to my Critics", 689.

11 Paul Mendes-Flohr, Preface to *Martin Buber: A Contemporary Perspective*, ed. Paul Mendes-Flohr (Syracuse: Syracuse University Press and Jerusalem: The Israel Academy of Sciences and Humanities, 2002), VII.

12 Eliezer Berkovits, *A Jewish Critique of the Philosophy of Martin Buber (Studies in Torah Judaism)* (New York: Yeshiva University, 1962).

13 Hans Urs von Balthasar, "Martin Buber and Christianity", in *The Philosophy of Martin Buber*, eds. Paul Arthur Schilpp and Maurice Friedman (LaSalle, IL: Open Court, 1967), 341–360.

PLACE IN THE AUTHOR'S WORK

KEY POINTS

- *I and Thou* constitutes the first mature expression of Martin Buber's thought.

- There is debate around the degree of continuity across Buber's early and later work.

- There is no doubt that *I and Thou* is Buber's most significant publication.

Positioning

Prior to the publication of *I and Thou* in 1923, Buber had produced a variety of works. These include two volumes of re-written Hasidic legends, *The Tales of Rabbi Nachman* in 1906, and *The Legend of the Baal Shem* in 1908. He also wrote his first fully original philosophical book, *Daniel: Dialogues on Realization* in 1913. This anticipates aspects of *I and Thou* insofar as it distinguishes between two modes of human existence, foreshadowing the distinction he would later make between the attitudes of "I-Thou" and "I-It." In *Daniel*, Buber contrasts an "orienting" perspective—a detached, ordering attitude, linking experiences to one another according to one's goals—with a "realizing" one, in which one submerges oneself in an experience, and so grasps its full meaning and intensity.[1]

In *Daniel*, however, these attitudes remain inner and psychic (in the mind), rather than social and relational, as they would become in *I and Thou*. Indeed, Buber later regarded *Daniel* as simply a stepping stone on the way to *I and Thou* and for a long time refused to allow the publication of an English version "on the grounds that it did not represent his mature thought and thus might mislead his reader."[2]

> **❝** If I myself should designate something as the 'central portion of my life work,' then it could not be anything individual, but only the one basic insight that has led me...to an independent philosophical presentation: that the I-Thou relation to God and the I-Thou relation to one's fellow man are at bottom related to each other. **❞**
>
> Martin Buber, in Sydney and Beatrice Rome, *Philosophical Interrogations*

According to Buber, *I and Thou* constituted "the first mature expression of his thought."[3] It was, he said, the product of a vision that had been with him since his youth, but which had only by that point "reached steady clarity."[4] Buber spent the remainder of his life expanding upon his philosophy of dialogue. His subsequent work is made up primarily of defences, clarifications, and applications of this philosophy to other spheres, for example in the collection of essays, *Between Man and Man* (1947). It is notable that while these later works develop and apply the philosophical, theological, and social vision of *I and Thou*, they do not share its unique poetical form. In this sense, *I and Thou* remains distinctive even within Buber's own body of work for the way it combines style with philosophy.

Buber's other major project in the period after *I and Thou* was a new German translation of the entire Hebrew Bible. He had begun this with Franz Rosenzweig in 1925, and finally completed it in 1961. This itself made a unique contribution, albeit a very different one from *I and Thou*, in its attempt to recreate in German the original rhythm of the Hebrew. It has been described as much a work of "interpretation and commentary" as one of simple translation.[5]

Integration

There has been some debate as to the degree of continuity between the writings which precede *I and Thou* and those that follow. In this regard, a distinction is made by many Buber scholars between an early "mystical" stage in Buber's thinking and his main "dialogical" stage, beginning with *I and Thou*. Buber himself spoke of a "conversion" or "transformation" in his own thought in this respect.[6] The key shift is said to have occurred around the time of World War I between the publication of *Daniel* and *I and Thou*. The real extent of this shift is debatable, however.

Commentators such as Ernst Simon* have argued there is a strict distinction between the two stages and others, like Gershom Scholem* and more recently Israel Koren*, have made a case for much greater continuity.[7] Others, such as Rivka Horwitz, Maurice Friedman, Avraham Shapira, and to some extent Paul Mendes-Flohr occupy a middle position, arguing for elements of continuity and discontinuity.[8] Koren has concluded that the varying positions of Buber scholars on this matter seems to depend more on their definition of mysticism than their specific readings of Buber's work.[9]

This seems to make the issue more one of categorization than interpretation. Most see at least some substantial break between the two stages of Buber's work. Koren suggests this relies on an extreme definition of mysticism including the total negation of the self. However, this is an idea that can certainly not be found in *I and Thou* and Koren says it cannot actually be found in *Daniel* either. "If we adopt a more moderate definition of the mystical phenomenon," he says, "then both works [*Daniel* and *I and Thou*] will be found to express a philosophical-mystic outlook."[10] Even if one disagrees with Koren's definition of mysticism, however, it is still possibility to see continuity across Buber's early and later writings. A close analysis of these indicates, as Shapira has said, that many of the "tendencies and patterns of [Buber's] thought were firmly established" before *I and Thou*.[11]

Significance

Regardless of one's position in this debate, it is certain that the publication of *I and Thou* marked a pivotal moment in Buber's career. It permanently established his reputation as one of the foremost philosophical and religious thinkers of the twentieth century. Most of his later work was spent deepening and applying the philosophy first explored in those pages. Even if some of these works, such as *Between Man and Man*, can be said to have had their own specific influence because of their more conventional academic form, there can be no doubt that *I and Thou* is Buber's most important contribution overall.

Buber involved himself in a variety of projects over the course of his life, including the retelling of Hasidic legends and a new translation of the Hebrew Bible, and he wrote across a wide variety of disciplines. He is nevertheless most closely associated with the idea of the I-Thou relation. His thought centers on this idea and the exploration of its wider implications across the many spheres of human individual and social life. Any reflection on his career must, therefore, begin and end with the philosophy of dialogue put forward in *I and Thou*.

NOTES

1   Maurice Friedman, *Martin Buber: The Life of Dialogue*, 4th edn. (London: Routledge, 2002), 41.

2   Maurice Friedman, *Encounter on the Narrow Ridge: A Life of Martin Buber* (New York: Paragon House, 1991), 72.

3   Friedman, *Encounter on the Narrow Ridge*, ix.

4   Martin Buber, 1957 Postscript to *I and Thou*, trans. Ronald Gregor-Smith, 2nd edn. (Edinburgh: T&T Clark, 1958), 155.

5   Lawrence Rosenwald, "On the Reception of Buber and Rosenzweig's Bible", *Prooftexts* 14 (1994), 165.

6   Martin Buber, "Autobiographical Fragments", in *The Philosophy of Martin Buber*, edited by Paul Arthur Schilpp and Maurice Friedman (LaSalle, IL: Open Court, 1967), 25-26; Shapira, *Hope For Our Time*, 5.

7   Israel Koren, *The Mystery of the Earth: Mysticism and Hasidism in the Thought of Martin Buber* (Leiden: Koninklijke Brill NV, 2010).

8   Israel Koren, "Between Buber's *Daniel* and His *I and Thou*: A New Examination", *Modern Judaism* 22 (2002), 169–98.

9   Koren, "Between Buber's *Daniel* and His *I and Thou*", 191.

10 Koren, "Between Buber's *Daniel* and His *I and Thou*", 191-192.

11 Avraham Shapira, *Hope For Our Time: Key Trends In The Thought of Martin Buber*, trans. Jeffrey M. Green (Albany, NY: State University of New York Press, 1999), 5–6.

SECTION 3
IMPACT

MODULE 9
THE FIRST RESPONSES

KEY POINTS

- The most important criticisms of *I and Thou* questioned Buber's division of human existence into two modes.
- Buber regarded many criticisms of his work to be based on misunderstandings.
- Buber did not change his views significantly due to criticism, but did seek to clarify his meaning.

Criticism

Martin Buber's *I and Thou* received criticism from a wide variety of perspectives in the years after publication.[1] The most fundamental criticisms have concerned whether Buber's division of existence into just two modes, I-It and I-Thou, does justice to the complexity of human engagement with the world. Walter Kaufmann claimed, for example, that human reality is not "twofold," as Buber suggests but "manifold," and that Buber's account was therefore reductive and simplified.[2] Emil Fackenheim* argued a similar point, suggesting that there should be a third mode between these two attitudes.[3]

A related question concerns the status of the I-It. For instance, Franz Rosenzweig, a friend and colleague of Buber, thought that while Buber attended admirably to the "Thou" in his book, he "wrongs the It": for Rosenzweig, the "I-It" appears as little more than a "cripple" in Buber's presentation, set up merely as an "antagonist" for the higher I-Thou relation.[4] Buber thereby fails properly to recognize the importance of the "It" attitude.

A further criticism concerned Buber's claim that the I-Thou relation, which is one of mutuality and dialogue, can come into being

> **❝** ...many readers are not trained to think either dialectically or phenomenologically, and for this reason they want to read Buber's polar terms as incompatible opposites, as either/ors between which one must choose. This has been as great an obstacle to the understanding of his thought, even by scholars, philosophers, and theologians, as any other single factor. **❞**
>
> Maurice Friedman, *Encounter on the Narrow Ridge*

not only between persons, but also between persons and nature, and persons and God or spirit.[5] The question raised was how these two latter forms of relation could be properly dialogical in the way an inter-human relation can be.

Responses

The majority of Martin Buber's responses to critics of *I and Thou* consisted either of rebuttals or, if he felt he had been misunderstood, clarifications. Kaufman and Fackenheim, for instance, argued that his core distinction between I-It and I-Thou did not account for the full diversity of human experience. Buber responded that he did not mean that these modes were exhaustive: "I by no means hold human 'inner life' in general, and within it human thinking in particular, to be exclusively composed of occurrences of the one and the other kinds."[6] Only when a person "presents himself to the world, or in general to others," he says, is it "either the one I or the other."[7] While Buber is insistent on this last point, his explanation that the I–Thou and I–It attitudes are not, for him, exhaustive of human inner life was significant.

In response to Rosenzweig's criticism that he failed to give proper attention to the I–it attitude, Buber argued that this was a matter of emphasis rather than an actual flaw in his argument. Had he been writing at a different time and place, he may have been able to "sound the praises of the It," he said.[8] As it was, the urgency that he felt was to draw special attention to the relation of I and Thou.

Buber provided a substantial response to critics who had queried his claim that mutuality could arise not only in the personal sphere, but also between people and nature or spirit. His Postscript added to a later edition of *I and Thou* developed his argument regarding the human relation to nature by dividing it into two further levels. He describes a "liminal" relationship possible with animals – "liminal" insofar as it is on the threshold of language, incorporating elements of spontaneity that come close to mutuality; and a "pre-liminal" relationship with the rest of nature, which is non-verbal.[9]

Conflict and Consensus

No criticism of *I and Thou* ever caused Buber substantially to modify his views, and he always defended the book's basic ideas. Primarily because of its style, *I and Thou* is a difficult work to interpret and therefore many criticisms of it arose, in his view, from misunderstandings. Indeed, Buber described one of the most comprehensive engagements with his work, *The Philosophy of Martin Buber*, which included an impressive array of 30 essays from leading scholars, as representing "the whole range of possible misunderstandings of his thought."[10]

He did, however, work to clarify his meaning in the face of such misunderstandings. One area where he did acknowledge that his original presentation was confusing was with respect to the I-Thou relationship with nature. Had he written the book again, he said that "he would not deny the I-Thou relationship with nature but neither would he use the same terminology for the relationship between person and person and that between man and nature."[11]

As the debate over *I and Thou* has progressed, a central question has remained: was Buber's characterization of human existence divided between I–Thou and I–It modes appropriate or accurate? Buber's "polarized" way of thinking—his habit of thinking in opposite pairs, as here—is characteristic, and, as Friedman has put it, is what gives his thought "elasticity and subtlety."[12] At the same time, it has continued to be "the occasion of misunderstanding and confusion" because of the tendency for readers to think of Buber's pairs as "incompatible opposites."[13]

NOTES

1   For a large collection of such responses, see Paul Arthur Schilpp and Maurice Friedman, eds., *The Philosophy of Martin Buber* (LaSalle, IL: Open Court, 1967).

2   Walter Kaufman, "I and You: A Prologue," in Martin Buber, *I and Thou*, trans. Walter Kaufman (Edinburgh: T&T Clark, 1970), 9–48.

3   Emil Fackenheim, "Buber's Concept of Revelation", in *The Philosophy of Martin Buber*, eds. Paul Arthur Schilpp and Maurice Friedman (LaSalle, IL: Open Court, 1967), 292.

4   Letter from Rosenzweig, cited in Martin Buber, *The Letters of Martin Buber: A Life of Dialogue*, ed. Nahum N. Glatzer and Paul Mendes-Flohr (Syracuse, NY: Syracuse University Press, 1996), 278.

5   Nathan Rotenstreich, "The Right and the Limitations of Buber's Dialogical Thought", in *The Philosophy of Martin Buber*, eds. Paul Arthur Schilpp and Maurice Friedman (LaSalle, IL: Open Court, 1967), 105-109; Fackenheim, "Buber's Concept of Revelation", 292-296.

6   Martin Buber, "Replies to my Critics", in *The Philosophy of Martin Buber*, ed. Paul Arthur Schilpp and Maurice Friedman (LaSalle, IL: Open Court, 1967), 691.

7   Buber, "Replies to my Critics", 691.

8   Buber, "Replies to my Critics," 704.

9   Buber, 1957 Postscript to *I and Thou*, 155-171.

10 Quoted in Maurice Friedman, *Encounter on the Narrow Ridge: A Life of Martin Buber* (New York: Paragon House, 1991), 379.

11 Friedman, *Encounter on the Narrow Ridge,* 130 cf. 378.

12 Friedman, *Encounter on the Narrow Ridge*, 350.

13 Friedman, *Encounter on the Narrow Ridge*, 350.

MODULE 10
THE EVOLVING DEBATE

KEY POINTS

- Buber built on the insights of *I and Thou* in subsequent works, without significantly changing them.

- Buber's ideas have had an extremely wide and general influence across many different fields.

- Maurice Friedman has been the most notable upholder of Buber's ideas and legacy since his death.

Uses and Problems

In the first decades after the publication of *I and Thou*, much of Buber's work was committed to making what he called "additions" in "independent form" to it.[1] These were collected and published in 1947 as *Between Man and Man* and included essays developing Buber's notion of dialogue and his philosophical anthropology, particularly in a long essay entitled "What Is Man?"[2] The latter is an interesting development of the anthropological insights of *I and Thou*. Written in a more conventional academic fashion, it takes the form of direct conversations with the views of other philosophers, including Kant, Marx, and Nietzsche. Still at the heart of these discussions, however, was, as Buber later put it, "the close connexion of the relation to God with the relation to one's fellow man."[3]

Later volumes include *The Eclipse of God* (1952), which broadly argues that the subjectivism* of modern thought has obstructed our view of God and our consciousness of His presence. It features an important essay attacking the ideas of Jean-Paul Sartre,* Martin Heidegger, and Carl Jung* for contributing to the "eclipse of God."[4] *The Knowledge of Man* (1965) features Buber's most mature and

> **❝** Buber's thought is universally known and has
> exercised a tremendous influence throughout the
> world. **❞**
>
> Emmanuel Levinas,* "On Buber"

technical philosophical writing, most notably the essay "Distance
and Relation." Buber had argued in *I and Thou* that from the
perspective of the human person existing in the world (that is, from an
anthropological perspective) relation is fundamental and primordial.
In this essay, however, he argues that, from the perspective of being or
existence as such (that is, from an ontological perspective), the reverse
is the case, and distance takes precedence over relation.[5] Here, and in
each of the works mentioned above, Buber was deepening and
supplementing the philosophical ideas first put forward in *I and Thou*,
without meaningfully departing from them.

Buber died in 1967, but in the decades since his death many of the
work's key concepts—particularly the I-Thou relation—have been
absorbed, in the particular sense that Buber meant them, into the
discourses of philosophy, theology, and numerous other disciplines,
including psychology and psychotherapy, aesthetic and literary theory,
political and economic thought, and education.[6] As Steven T. Katz*
has commented: "Everywhere that sophisticated individuals try to
understand the human condition and to decipher the diverse forms of
interaction that human beings are capable of, Buber's thought and
distinctive language influences, enriches and illuminates the
conversation."[7]

Schools of Thought

Martin Buber's *I and Thou* is one of the best known and most
influential texts of twentieth-century religious philosophy, and Buber
himself is arguably the most famous Jewish philosopher of his

generation. Even so, he cannot be said to have given birth to a specific school of thought or a distinctive group of followers that define themselves as "Buberian." His influence has been far broader and more disparate than that and crosses a range of disciplines.

With regard to Buber's influence on modern Jewish thought, Gershom Scholem has said that "we have all been Buber's students."[8] Recent works further exploring Buber's thought from a Jewish perspective include those by Avraham Shapira and Israel Koren.[9] In terms of western philosophy, Buber's notion of dialogue and the ontology* that underpins it has continued to be studied as an original and important intervention.[10] More recently, Buber has also been studied alongside other major twentieth-century philosophers, such as Emmanuel Levinas and Martin Heidegger, so as to better understand how their respective ideas relate.[11]

I and Thou has also had a substantial influence on Christian (especially Protestant) theology and the work of theologians such as Karl Barth* and Paul Tillich* and their followers.[12] Others have sought to apply the principles of Buber's thought to new areas in ways that are faithful to his original ideas. One example of this is the psychotherapist John C. Gunzburg* in his book, *Healing Through Meeting: Martin Buber's Conversational Approach To Psychotherapy*.[13] Ronald C. Arnett* did the same in the field of communication studies.[14] In these cases, the principles of dialogue found originally in *I and Thou* form the thematic and conceptual basis of a new and much broader field of study.

In Current Scholarship

Until his death in 2012, the most prolific and faithful proponent of Buber's work in the English-speaking world was Maurice Friedman. Over the course of many years, he wrote and edited numerous volumes devoted to Buber's thought, including his monumental, three-volume biography, *Martin Buber's Life and Work*.[15] Friedman did more than anybody else to continue the critical conversations on Buber and to highlight and develop his legacy. Friedman also sought to apply Buber's philosophy of dialogue to the discourse between psychology and religion,–for example, in his 1992 publication, *Religion and Psychology: A Dialogical Approach.*[16]

Another contemporary "disciple" of Buber is his former student, the sociologist and economist Amitai Etzioni.* Inspired by Buber, Etzioni has sought to develop a better way of thinking about economics, one that attends more fully to the social dimension of economic activity. He refers to Buber as his "Master–teacher" and the source of the philosophical foundations of his work, which lie in what he calls "responsive community."[17] Etzioni is an example of someone who has used Buber's insights into the human condition to criticize the anthropological assumptions of another discipline, in this case economics.

NOTES

1   Martin Buber, 1957 Postscript to *I and Thou*, trans. Ronald Gregor-Smith, 2nd edn. (Edinburgh: T&T Clark, 1958), 155.

2   Martin Buber, *Between Man and Man*, trans. Ronald Gregor Smith (London: Routledge and Kegan Paul, 1947), 118-205.

3   Buber, 1957 Postscript to *I and Thou*, 155.

4   Martin Buber, *The Eclipse of God: Studies in the Relation Between Religion and Philosophy* (New York: Prometheus Books, 1988), 63-92.

5   Martin Buber, *The Knowledge of Man: Selected Essays* (New York: Harper and Row, 1965), 59-71.

6   See, for instance, Maurice Friedman, ed., *Martin Buber and the Human Sciences* (Albany, NY: State University of New York Press, 1996), and Michael Zank, ed., *New Perspectives on Martin Buber* (Tübingen: Mohr Siebeck, 2003).

7   Steven T. Katz, "Martin Buber in Retrospect", in *New Perspectives on Martin Buber*, edited by Michael Zank (Tübingen: Mohr Siebeck, 2003), 261.

8   Cited in Zank, Introduction to *New Perspectives on Martin Buber*, 2.

9   Avraham Shapira, *Hope For Our Time: Key Trends In The Thought of Martin Buber*, trans. Jeffrey M. Green (Albany, NY: State University of New York Press, 1999); Israel Koren, *The Mystery of the Earth: Mysticism and Hasidism in the Thought of Martin Buber* (Leiden: Koninklijke Brill NV, 2010).

10   See for example, Robert E. Wood, *Martin Buber's Ontology: An Analysis of I and Thou* (Evanston: Northwestern University Press, 1969).

11   Peter Atterton, Matthew Calarco, and Maurice Friedman, eds, *Levinas and Buber: Dialogue and Difference* (Pittsburgh, PA: Duquesne University Press, 2004); Haim Gordon, *The Heidegger-Buber Controversy: The Status of the I–Thou* (Westport, CN: Greenwood, 2001).

12   Maurice Friedman, *Martin Buber: The Life of Dialogue*, 4th edn. (London: Routledge, 2002), 319-333.

13   John C. Gunzburg, *Healing Through Meeting: Martin Buber's Conversational Approach To Psychotherapy* (London: Jessica Kingsley, 1997).

14   Ronald C. Arnett, *Communication and Community: Implications of Martin Buber's Dialogue* (Carbondale and Edwardsville: Southern Illinois University Press, 1986).

15   Maurice Friedman, *Martin Buber's Life and Work*, 3 vols. (Detroit, MI: Wayne State University Press, 1988).

16   Maurice Friedman, *Religion and Psychology: A Dialogical Approach* (New York: Paragon House, 1992).

17   Amitai Etzioni, *The Moral Dimension: Towards A New Economics* (New York, NY: Simon and Schuster, 1990), 8.

MODULE 11
IMPACT AND INFLUENCE TODAY

KEY POINTS

- *I and Thou* is considered a classic work of twentieth-century religious philosophy.

- Buber's thought continues to generate substantial responses across a variety of fields.

- It has, however, become possible to ignore the challenge that his ideas still pose to contemporary thinking.

Position

Martin Buber's *I and Thou* "catapulted him to international fame"[1] and is widely considered a classic of twentieth-century philosophy. Its themes and key terms, such as the "I–Thou relation," have been absorbed into the broad intellectual culture of western society, as well as Jewish thought. However, it is precisely this level of familiarity that raises the question of whether, in the present day, Buber remains relevant or whether he has become merely an artefact of history.[2] Buber's ideas are certainly no longer at the forefront of philosophical thought. Academic fashions change and many more contemporary names have come and gone since his death.

Moreover, the sheer range of Buber's work, crossing over boundaries into many academic fields, can itself pose problems. To quote Shapira: "Some of [Buber's] writings are called 'Biblical', 'Hasidic', 'sociological', 'philosophical', 'theological', 'sociopolitical', etc. But the majority of them do not have a disciplinary or professional character."[3] It can be unclear, given this, which discipline is best placed to curate Buber's scholarly legacy.

> ❝ His poetical philosophical classic *I and Thou* is universally recognised as one of the most influential books of the twentieth century...[his] philosophy of dialogue...has had a revolutionary impact on Christian and Jewish theology and religious thought in our time, and it has an ever growing influence on aesthetics, psychology and psychotherapy, education, speech communication, sociology, and social thought. ❞
>
> Maurice Friedman, *Martin Buber and the Human Sciences*

For these reasons, scholarly engagement with Buber has cooled off in recent decades, though his work has continued to provoke new reflections across a surprising array of fields. Maurice Friedman's 1996 collection looks broadly at Buber's ongoing impact on the human sciences, including essays from within philosophy and religion, aesthetics and literature, economics, politics and history, and psychological practice.[4] Paul Mendes-Flohr's 2002 edited volume critically assesses Buber's contribution to some of the many academic disciplines with which he engaged, and includes essays by high-profile names including Rémi Brague* and the late Gillian Rose.*[5] Michael Zank's* 2006 volume features new essays re-examining Buber's work from aesthetic, philosophical, biblical, and political perspectives.[6]

In addition, examples of constructive new interpretations of Buber's work have recently appeared from the likes of Avraham Shapira, who has proposed that it is not the idea of dialogue but the "binary nature" of Buber's thought, centered on principles of polarity and duality, that should be said to constitute its real "hidden scaffolding."[7] A further new intervention has come from Israel Koren, who has argued, against the prevailing view, for the continuity of the "mystical" and "dialogical" phases of Buber's thought.[8] The continued relevance of the principles presented in *I and Thou* to contemporary life, even outside academia, is borne out by the recent publication of a new overview of Buber's philosophy of dialogue for the popular market.[9]

Interaction

The ideas contained in *I and Thou* still present important challenges to some of the dominant ways of engaging with and conceiving the world in the twenty-first century. Many disciplines still assume a detached, asocial idea of what it is to be human and this can neglect the relational dimension of human existence that Buber sought to highlight in his work. One example of this is the discipline of economics, at least in its mainstream form. As Mark A. Lutz* has remarked, because of its narrow and abstract assumptions about the human subject, economics has more need of interaction with Buber's thought that any other social science. "Only by starting to recognize a Dialogical Person side-by-side with Logical Man," he remarks, "can the discipline be expected to appreciate the increasingly scarce value of genuine community."[10] As mentioned in the last module, part of Amitai Etzioni's work has also moved in this direction in recent decades.

Another of the central concerns of *I and Thou* that still has clear contemporary relevance is what Buber later called the "eclipse of God." As Donald J. Moore* has put it, "Authentic faith and authentic humanity can never be divorced in Buber's thought."[11] Much contemporary philosophy continues to reject any notion of transcendence* in a way that Buber would have felt closes us off from the presence of God in the I-Thou relation. Buber also called into question forms of theology that reduce God to a concept (one who is spoken *about* rather than one who is *addressed*). This remains a challenge to contemporary theology, particularly in the form of its speech about God. As Moore puts it with respect to his own tradition, "There is a growing realization the Buber represents for Catholic thought a profound challenge."[12]

The Continuing Debate

Most of today's substantial responses to Buber come from scholars who are already sympathetic to his core ideas and who regard it as useful and relevant to their own intellectual interests, even if they are working out of a different tradition or discipline. As such, although the themes of *I and Thou* can be said to pose a wide intellectual challenge in many respects, it has become possible–simply because Buber is no longer a very contemporary voice–to ignore this challenge. Moore, for example, engages constructively with Buber because he is already convinced of the importance of the challenge Buber poses to his own Catholic tradition.

Similarly, Lutz is convinced of the value of Buber's thought on the anthropological assumptions made my mainstream economists, and so engages with him on that level, as has Amitai Etzioni. By contrast, as Lutz puts it, it is "painfully obvious that his influence among pure economic theorists has been essentially nil."[13] The continuing debate that Buber's work inspires, therefore, is mostly carried on not by his opponents but by relatively sympathetic voices, even if they then wish to go beyond or critique Buber in some way (as with Brague and Rose).[14] This is, however, not unusual for a book at this stage in its reception.

NOTES

1   Steven T. Katz, "Martin Buber in Retrospect", in *New Perspectives on Martin Buber*, edited by Michael Zank (Tübingen: Mohr Siebeck, 2003), 261.

2   Michael Zank, Introduction to *New Perspectives on Martin Buber*, edited by Michael Zank (Tübingen: Mohr Siebeck, 2003), 1–2.

3   Avraham Shapira, *Hope For Our Time: Key Trends In The Thought of Martin Buber*, trans. Jeffrey M. Green (Albany, NY: State University of New York Press, 1999), 195.

4   Maurice Friedman, ed., *Martin Buber and the Human Sciences* (Albany, NY: State University of New York Press, 1996).

5   Paul Mendes-Flohr (ed.), *Martin Buber: A Contemporary Perspective* (Syracuse: Syracuse University Press and Jerusalem: The Israel Academy of Sciences and Humanities, 2002),

6   Michael Zank (ed.), *New Perspectives on Martin Buber* (Tübingen: Mohr Siebeck, 2003).

7   Shapira, *Hope For Our Time*, 197.

8   Israel Koren, *The Mystery of the Earth: Mysticism and Hasidism in the Thought of Martin Buber* (Leiden: Koninklijke Brill NV, 2010).

9   Kenneth Paul Kraemer with Mechthild Gawlick, *Martin Buber's "I and Thou": Practicing Living Dialogue* (Mahwah, NJ: Paulist Press, 2003).

10 Mark A. Lutz, "The Relevance of Martin Buber's Philosophical Anthropology for Economic Thought," in *Martin Buber and the Human Sciences*, ed. Maurice Friedman (Albany, NY: State University of New York Press, 1996), 278-279.

11 Donald J. Moore SJ, "Martin Buber and Christian Theology: A Continuing Dialogue", in *Martin Buber and the Human Sciences*, ed. Maurice Friedman (Albany, NY: State University of New York Press, 1996), 94.

12 Moore, "Martin Buber and Christian Theology", 99.

13 Lutz, "The Relevance of Martin Buber's Philosophical Anthropology", 278.

14 Rémi Brague, "How to Be in the World: Gnosis, Religion, Philosophy", in *Martin Buber: A Contemporary Perspective*, ed. Paul Mendes-Flohr (Syracuse: Syracuse University Press and Jerusalem: The Israel Academy of Sciences and Humanities, 2002), 133-147; Gillian Rose, "Reply from 'The Single One': Soren Kierkegaard to Martin Buber", in *Martin Buber: A Contemporary Perspective*, ed. Paul Mendes-Flohr (Syracuse: Syracuse University Press and Jerusalem: The Israel Academy of Sciences and Humanities, 2002), 148-165.

WHERE NEXT?

KEY POINTS

- Buber's description of the I-Thou relation has relevance for contemporary debates on the nature of human happiness.

- New applications of Buber's ideas may be more likely to come from disciplines outside philosophy and theology.

- *I and Thou*'s unique emphasis on the importance of dialogue and relationship give it lasting appeal.

Potential

Buber once wrote that he had no "teaching," by which he meant that his work did not try to convince people of an academic argument, but instead simply existed to "point to something in reality that had not or had too little been seen."[1] The relational dimension of human existence to which Buber pointed, and which we have explored in this analysis lies, on his account, beyond formal reasoning, measurement, or classification. It is not an item of knowledge to be held in the mind, like an abstract fact, but something that must be acted upon and lived out if it is to be known.

"Love is *between* I and Thou," Buber emphasized, meaning that it was not to be found in the mind or in one's inner feelings, but out in the world, with others.[2] Buber was convinced that being open to this deep, relational dimension of existence was vital if humans were to flourish. Being closed off to it would mean living only in the I-It attitude and lead to "nothingness."[3]

Much attention has been given in recent years to questions of happiness and wellbeing, including how they can be accurately measured. Governments and public bodies now refer to wellbeing

> **❝** Buber's key teaching–consistent with Buber's own exposition, I do not call it a doctrine or philosophy–remains a vital, life-altering message today, just as it was...when *Ich und Du* was first published. **❞**
>
> Steven T. Katz, "Martin Buber in Retrospect"

indexes to gauge the progress of society towards happiness. As William Davies* has shown, this project is rooted in utilitarian* ideas that have tended to think of happiness as a measurable quantity.[4] Buber, however, would consider this to be based on a terrible misunderstanding. Human happiness is for Buber something that comes out of our relationships with others, those we address personally as Thou. To treat happiness as something that can be measured is to think of it only in terms of an "It"–an object that we can manipulate. This attitude is quite different from that needed truly to meet others, in a spirit of dialogue and openness.

That there is still confusion around these kinds of issues shows the ongoing relevance of Buber's *I and Thou*, nearly a hundred years after its publication. Buber's text is considered a classic work, with an established place in the history of philosophical and religious thought, but it would be unfortunate if that meant that it no longer played a role in present-day debates around the nature of human happiness. There is no reason why, albeit alongside the work of many others, it should not.

Future Directions

No one would expect scholars to follow Buber's scheme in its entirety and nor was that his intention (as indicated by his remark about having no "teaching," above). Rather, anywhere where his core idea is recognized–the importance of relation, beyond that which is useful, measurable, or manipulable–his legacy can be said to live on. As we have seen, Buber's central ideas have in recent years been received in new ways and in disciplines beyond philosophy and theology, including aesthetic* and literary theory, psychology and psychotherapy, education, politics, and economics. If over-familiarity with *I and Thou* among scholars in its immediate fields of philosophy and theology means that its ongoing relevance is less easily recognized there, it may be that it will increasingly be taken up in these newer disciplines.

The generation of thinkers that came after Buber and took his legacy into the twenty-first century, including the late Maurice Friedman and Amitai Etzioni, have reached or are reaching the end of their own careers and lives. Now a new generation is needed to take on Buber's ideas in the decades ahead if they are to be applied in new ways to contemporary problems. While we cannot be sure precisely who the leaders of that new generation may be, the vision at the heart *I and Thou* remains significant and it seems certain that its message will continue to be heard.

Summary

I and Thou explores in a new way the structure of human existence, divided between I-It and I-Thou attitudes. Buber distinguishes between these two modes and argues that inhabiting the I-Thou relation is what makes a person fully human. He goes on to offer a subtle critique both of prevailing philosophical accounts of the human as solitary, and also of his wider society, for neglecting this deep relational dimension of human life. The detached attitude of the I-It is indeed important for many material reasons, according to Buber, but it is not in his view enough on its own to make human life meaningful. The way the book calls attention to the importance of the social and communal aspects of human existence is in this way unique and compelling. Buber also infuses human social relationships with spiritual significance by explaining how they bring us into contact with God: "In every *Thou* we address the eternal *Thou*."[5]

For these reasons, the work has had long-term influence, bringing renewed attention to the themes of dialogue and relation across many academic fields, as well as beyond academia. *I and Thou* is the thematic and conceptual heart of Buber's broader philosophy and the basis of his legacy. It continues to compel its readers to reflect critically on their assumptions about the structure of human existence, and to consider the fundamental question of what it is that makes life worth living. The universal nature of this question, and the profound and humane way in which Buber himself answered it, is what explains the book's ongoing appeal well into the twenty-first century.

NOTES

1 Martin Buber, "Replies to my Critics", in *The Philosophy of Martin Buber*, ed. Paul Arthur Schilpp and Maurice Friedman (LaSalle, IL: Open Court, 1967), 693.

2 Martin Buber, *I and Thou*, trans. Ronald Gregor-Smith, 2nd edn (Edinburgh: T&T Clark, 1958), 28.

3 Buber, *I and Thou*, 40.

4 William Davies, *The Happiness Industry: How the Government and Big Business Sold Us Wellbeing* (London: Verso, 2015).

5 Buber, *I and Thou*, 19.

GLOSSARY

GLOSSARY OF TERMS

Aesthetics: the branch of philosophy concerned with the nature and perception of beauty.

Aphorism: a short and concise passage of text, conveying usually a single insight.

Creatio ex nihilo: a theological doctrine that teaches that the world was created by God out of nothing.

Capitalism: an economic system based upon private ownership of the means of production and their operation for profit, with private property, competitive markets, and waged labor as central features.

Copernican Revolution: the drastic shift in thinking that took place in the sixteenth century from the view that the earth was at the center of the universe, to the view that the earth orbits around the sun.

Dasein: a concept in the philosophy of Martin Heidegger. It literally means "being-there" in German, but refers to the kind of being in the world that is peculiar to humans.

Dialogical philosophy/philosophy of dialogue: a philosophy for which the central focus is that of the relation between the self and others.

The Enlightenment: an intellectual and cultural movement of the seventeenth and eighteenth centuries that helped to shape the principles (especially those of reason, science and the individual) on which modern societies are based.

Existentialism: a philosophical approach originating in the nineteenth century that prioritizes the lived existence of the individual in the world.

Fascism: a system of authoritarian government where power is centralized under a dictator, political opposition is disallowed, and national (and often racial) identity is given central significance over that of the individual or minority groups.

Fin de siècle: a French term meaning "end of the century," but referring most commonly to the period of cultural change towards the end of the nineteenth century.

Hapsburg Empire: the countries and provinces that were ruled by the Houses of Hapsburg (Austrian branch) and Hapsburg-Lorraine from the early sixteenth to the early twentieth centuries, with a capital for most of that time in Vienna.

Hasidism: a form of mystical Judaism that originated with the Rabbi Baal Shem Tov, Israel Ben Eliezer (1700-1760), in Poland in the eighteenth century.

The Holocaust: the mass murder of more than six million European Jews, and members of other persecuted groups by Adolf Hitler's National Socialist regime during World War II.

Industrialization: the process whereby a society develops industries on a wide scale, usually for the purpose of mass manufacturing.

Metaphysics: the branch of philosophy that looks at fundamental questions regarding the basic structures of reality, such as the nature of space and time, existence, and the properties of objects.

Ontology: the branch pf philosophy that studies the nature of being.

Pantheism: a teaching that identifies God with nature and the universe.

Philosophical anthropology: the study of what constitutes the human person and the nature of their involvement in the world.

Psychoanalysis: a branch of psychology that seeks to identify and treat disorders by examining the way the conscious and unconscious mind interact.

Rabbinic literature: in its widest sense can refer to all writings by rabbis in Jewish history, but more commonly refers to those from the period before the medieval and modern era (known as the "Talmudic" era).

Subjectivism: a philosophical position arguing that the individual subject's reasoning is the only source of truth about the world, against any external or objective source.

Transcendence (theology): a term used to refer to the sphere of reality and of God's existence beyond human experience and perception, and beyond the material universe.

Utilitarianism: an ethical theory that states that the best course of action is always that which maximizes utility (utility itself may be defined in various ways).

World War I: a global war that began in Europe on 28 July 1914 and lasted until 11 November 1918, leading to the deaths of an estimated nine million military personnel and seven million civilians.

Zionism (before the settlement of Israel): a political movement for the re-establishment of a Jewish nation in Palestine.

PEOPLE MENTIONED IN THE TEXT

Ronald C. Arnett (born 1952) is a scholar of communication studies and rhetoric. He has written numerous books on dialogue, communications ethics, and the philosophy of communication, and is at the time of writing a professor in the Department of Communication & Rhetorical Studies at Duquesne University.

Hans Urs von Balthasar (1905–1988) was a Swiss theologian and Catholic priest. Considered one of the most important Catholic thinkers of the twentieth century and the author of many books, he is perhaps best known for his seven-volume work on theological aesthetics (the theology of beauty), entitled *The Glory of the Lord*.

Karl Barth (1886–1968) was a Swiss Reformed Protestant theologian. Best known for his multi-volume *Church Dogmatics*, Barth had a substantial influence on twentieth-century academic theology and on wider society, being featured on the cover of *Time* magazine in 1962.

Eliezer Berkovits (1908–1992) was an Orthodox Jewish theologian and rabbi. He wrote on numerous subjects across Jewish philosophy and thought, including a Jewish critique of Martin Buber.

Rémi Brague (born 1847) is a French historian of philosophy. He has written an influential trilogy of books on the philosophy of law in the history of the West, and is at the time of writing Professor Emeritus of Arabic and Religious Philosophy at the Sorbonne, and Romano Guardini Chair of Philosophy (Emeritus) at the Ludwig Maximilian University of Munich.

Emil Brunner (1889–1966) was a Swiss Protestant theologian. He is known for his three-volume dogmatic theology and, along with Karl Barth, for a new expression of orthodox Christian teaching known as "neo-orthodoxy."

Hermann Cohen (1842–1918) was a German-Jewish philosopher. He is often regarded as the most important Jewish philosopher of his generation due to his contributions reviving the work of Immanuel Kant (a school of thought known as "Neo-Kantianism"). He was also an opponent of Zionism.

William Davies is a British political economist. He has written on consumerism and happiness and is at the time of writing Reader in Political Economy at Goldsmiths College, University of London.

Wilhelm Dilthey (1833–1911) was a German philosopher. His most enduring contribution has been in thinking through the different methodologies of the natural and human sciences.

Fyodor Dostoevsky (1821–1881) was a Russian novelist. Often associated with existentialism, his books and stories explore troubling aspects of human psychology in a way that fuses literature with theological and philosophical concerns.

Ferdinand Ebner (1882–1931) was an Austrian Catholic teacher and philosopher. He was the author of numerous works in German, which developed a philosophy based on the principle of dialogue that has had considerable influence since his premature death.

Amitai Etzioni (born 1929) is an Israeli-American sociologist. He is best known for his work linking thinking on society to economics, and on communitarianism, a political philosophy that prioritizes shared communal interests over other factors. In 2001 he was named among the top 100 American intellectuals.

Emil Fackenheim (1916–2003) was a Jewish philosopher and rabbi. He explored questions around Jewish identity and the Jewish relation to God from a variety of philosophical and cultural perspectives.

Ludwig Feuerbach (1804–1872) was a German philosopher and anthropologist. He is best known for his critique of Christianity, which influenced later thinkers, and is found in his book *The Essence of Christianity*.

Sigmund Freud (1856–1939) was an Austrian neurologist. He was the founder of psychoanalysis both as a theory of human psychology and a clinical method for resolving psychological disorders or pathologies.

Maurice S. Friedman (1921–2012) was an interdisciplinary scholar of religion, philosophy, and psychology, whose work focused on the theme of dialogue. He translated, edited, and wrote numerous works on Martin Buber, including the definitive three-volume English biography, *Martin Buber's Life and Work*.

John C. Gunzburg is a psychotherapist. He has written books on different approaches to therapy, including an approach based on the philosophy of Martin Buber.

Dag Hammarskjöld (1905–1961) was a Swedish diplomat and economist. He served as the second Secretary-General of the United Nations from 1953 until his death in 1961. Shortly after his death he was awarded the Nobel Peace Prize, an award for which he had nominated Martin Buber in 1959.

Martin Heidegger (1889–1976) was a German philosopher. He is acknowledged to have been one of the most influential thinkers of the twentieth century, and is best known for his early work *Being and Time*, a new investigation of the nature of Being.

Adolf Hitler (1889–1945) was a German Fascist politician and Chancellor of Germany from 1933 to 1945. As a dictator, Hitler initiated World War II in Europe as well as the mass killing of millions of Jews known as the Holocaust.

Rivka Horwitz (1926–2007) was an Israeli philosopher. She was Professor of Philosophy and Jewish Thought at the Ben-Gurion University of the Negev, and was known for her work on Franz Rosenzweig and Martin Buber.

Carl Jung (1875–1961) was a Swiss psychiatrist and psychoanalyst. He is the founder of the psychological and therapeutic method known as analytical psychology, often distinguished from that of Sigmund Freud.

Immanuel Kant (1724–1804) was a German philosopher. He made decisive and fundamental contributions to modern philosophy with works such as *The Critique of Pure Reason* and *The Critique of Practical Reason*.

Steven T. Katz (born 1944) is a Jewish philosopher. He has written many books, particularly on themes in Jewish mysticism, and is at the time of writing Alvin J. and Shirley Slater Chair in Jewish Holocaust Studies at Boston University.

Walter Kaufman (1921–1980) was a German-American philosopher, author, and translator. He translated and commented upon many key works of modern European philosophy, including those by Friedrich Nietzsche and Martin Buber.

Søren Kierkegaard (1813–1855) was a Danish philosopher and Christian theologian. He is considered the first existentialist philosopher and much of his work concerns the problem of how to live as a "single individual."

Israel Koren is a Senior Lecturer of Jewish mysticism, Jewish Education and Jewish Modern thought at Oranim College of Education and David Yellin College of Education in Israel. He has published articles and a book on modern Jewish mysticism.

Emmanuel Levinas (1906–1995) was a French–Jewish philosopher. He is known for his notion of ethics as "first philosophy," centered on the face-to-face encounter with the Other.

Mark A. Lutz (born 1941) is Swiss-born economist. His work has focused on arguing for a more humane approach to the discipline of economics, most notably in his book *Economics for the Common Good*.

Gabriel Marcel (1889–1973) was a French Christian philosopher. Marcel was an existentialist who contrasted "being" and "having" as opposing ways of being human, and is well known for his two-volume *The Mystery of Being*.

Karl Marx (1818–1883) was a philosopher, economist, historian, and political theorist, born in Prussia (now Germany) but legally stateless after 1845. Much of his work focused on a detailed critique of capitalism and an argument for a revolution of the working classes, perhaps most famously in *The Communist Manifesto* of 1848.

Paul Mendes-Flohr (born 1941) is a scholar of modern Jewish thought. His research has focused on Jewish intellectual history, particularly the work of Gershom Scholem, Franz Rosenzweig, and Martin Buber. He is at the time of writing Dorothy Grant Maclear Professor of Modern Jewish History and Thought at the University of Chicago Divinity School.

Donald J. Moore SJ is a Catholic theologian. His published work has focused on facilitating conversation between Catholic and Jewish theology.

Friedrich Nietzsche (1844–1900) was a German philosopher. He made important critiques of contemporary philosophy, morality, and religion on the basis of an interpretation of the human desire for power, that have had significant influence in the twentieth century.

Gillian Rose (1947–1995) was a British philosopher. She is best known for her critical engagement with nineteenth and twentieth century European philosophy and her contributions to Jewish thought.

Franz Rosenzweig (1886–1929) was a German-Jewish religious philosopher. He is known for his account of dialogue, which influenced Martin Buber, and for his book *The Star of Redemption*.

Jean-Paul Sartre (1905–1980) was a French philosopher, playwright, and novelist. He argued in favor of existentialism in works such as *Being and Nothingness*, and has had a significant long-term impact on European philosophy.

Gershom Scholem (1897–1982) was a German-born Israeli philosopher and historian. His primary focus was on Jewish mysticism and he is widely regarded as the founder of the academic study of Kabbalah, a Jewish mystical school of thought.

Avraham Shapira is professor emeritus of Jewish Philosophy and Jewish History at Tel Aviv University. He has written on numerous important Jewish thinkers including A. D. Gordon, Gershom Scholem, and Martin Buber.

Georg Simmel (1858–1918) was a German sociologist and philosopher. He is best known for his contributions to sociological methodology, and for books including *The Philosophy of Money* and *The Metropolis and Mental Life.*

Ernst Akiba Simon (1899–1988) was a Jewish religious philosopher and educator. He was a close colleague of Martin Buber and in 1967 was awarded the Israel Prize for education.

Paul Tillich (1886–1965) was a German-American Protestant theologian and Christian existentialist. Thanks to his popular books *The Courage To Be* and *Dynamics of Faith*, as well as his three-volume *Systematic Theology*, he is often regarded as one of the foremost theologians of the twentieth century.

Michael Zank (born 1958) is a German-American theological scholar. He has worked especially on German-Jewish intellectual history, including the thought of Franz Rosenzweig, and is at the time of writing Director of the Elie Wiesel Center for Judaic Studies.

WORKS CITED

WORKS CITED

Arnett, Ronald C. *Communication and Community: Implications of Martin Buber's Dialogue*. Carbondale and Edwardsville: Southern Illinois University Press, 1986.

Atterton, Peter, Matthew Calarco, and Maurice Friedman, eds. *Levinas and Buber: Dialogue and Difference*. Pittsburgh, PA: Duquesne University Press, 2004.

Balthasar, Hans Urs von. "Martin Buber and Christianity". In *The Philosophy of Martin Buber*, edited by Paul Arthur Schilpp and Maurice Friedman, 341–60. LaSalle, IL: Open Court, 1967.

Berkovits, Eliezer. *A Jewish Critique of the Philosophy of Martin Buber (Studies in Torah Judaism)*. New York: Yeshiva University, 1962.

Brague, Rémi. "How to Be in the World: Gnosis, Religion, Philosophy". In *Martin Buber: A Contemporary Perspective*, edited by Paul Mendes-Flohr, 133-147. Syracuse: Syracuse University Press and Jerusalem: The Israel Academy of Sciences and Humanities, 2002.

Brunner, Emil. "Judaism and Christianity in Buber". In *The Philosophy of Martin Buber*, edited by Paul Arthur Schilpp and Maurice Friedman, 309-318. LaSalle, IL: Open Court, 1967.

Buber, Martin. *I and Thou*. 2nd edn. Translated by Ronald Gregor-Smith. Edinburgh: T&T Clark, 1958.

"Hope for this Hour". In *Pointing the Way: Collected Essays of Martin Buber*, edited by Maurice Friedman, 220-229. Evanston, IL: Harper Torchbooks, 1963.

Daniel: Dialogues on Realization. Translated by Maurice Friedman. Austin, TX: Holt, Rinehart and Winston, 1964.

The Knowledge of Man: Selected Essays. New York: Harper and Row, 1965.

"Autobiographical Fragments." In *The Philosophy of Martin Buber*, edited by Paul Arthur Schilpp and Maurice Friedman, 3-40. LaSalle, IL: Open Court, 1967.

"Replies to my Critics." In *The Philosophy of Martin Buber*, edited by Paul Arthur Schilpp and Maurice Friedman, 689–744. LaSalle, IL: Open Court, 1967.

The Eclipse of God: Studies in the Relation Between Religion and Philosophy. New York: Prometheus Books, 1988.

The Letters of Martin Buber: A Life of Dialogue. Edited by Nahum N. Glatzer and Paul Mendes-Flohr. Syracuse, NY: Syracuse University Press, 1996.

Between Man and Man. Translated by Ronald Gregor-Smith. London: Routledge and Kegan Paul, 1947.

Burrell, David B., Carlo Cogliati, Janet M. Soskice, and William R. Stoeger, eds. *Creation and the God of Abraham.* Cambridge: Cambridge University Press, 2010.

Davies, William. *The Happiness Industry: How the Government and Big Business Sold Us Wellbeing.* London: Verso, 2015.

Etzioni, Amitai. *The Moral Dimension: Towards A New Economics.* New York: Simon and Schuster, 1990.

Fackenheim, Emil. "Buber's Concept of Revelation". In *The Philosophy of Martin Buber*, eds. Paul Arthur Schilpp and Maurice Friedman, 273-296. LaSalle, IL: Open Court, 1967.

Friedman, Maurice. *Martin Buber and the Eternal.* New York: Human Sciences Press, 1986.

Martin Buber's Life and Work. 3 vols. Detroit, MI: Wayne State University Press, 1988.

Encounter on the Narrow Ridge: A Life of Martin Buber. New York: Paragon House, 1991.

Religion and Psychology: A Dialogical Approach. New York: Paragon House, 1992.

ed. *Martin Buber and the Human Sciences.* Albany, NY: State University of New York Press, 1996.

Martin Buber: The Life of Dialogue. 4th edn. London: Routledge, 2002.

Freud, Sigmund. *The Future of an Illusion.* Translated by W.D. Robson-Scott. London: Hogarth Press, 1953.

Gordon, Haim. *The Heidegger–Buber Controversy: The Status of the I–Thou.* Westport, CN: Greenwood, 2001.

Grainger, Roger. *Theatre and Relationship in Shakespeare's Later Plays.* Oxford: Peter Lang, 2008.

Gunzburg, John C. *Healing Through Meeting: Martin Buber's Conversational Approach To Psychotherapy.* London: Jessica Kingsley, 1997.

Heidegger, Martin. *Being and Time.* Translated by John Macquarrie and Edward Robinson. Oxford: Blackwell, 1962.

Horwitz, Rivka. *Buber's Way to "I and Thou": The Development of Martin Buber's Thought and His "Religion as Presence" Lectures.* New York: Jewish Publication Society, 1988.

Katz, Steven T. "Martin Buber in Retrospect". In *New Perspectives on Martin Buber*, edited by Michael Zank, 255–66. Tübingen: Mohr Siebeck, 2003.

Kaufman, Walter. "I and You: A Prologue". In Martin Buber, *I and Thou*, translated by Walter Kaufman, 9–48. Edinburgh: T&T Clark, 1970.

Koren, Israel. "Between Buber's Daniel and His *I and Thou*: A New Examination", *Modern Judaism* 22 (2002): 169–98.

The Mystery of the Earth: Mysticism and Hasidism in the Thought of Martin Buber. Leiden: Koninklijke Brill NV, 2010.

Kraemer, Kenneth Paul, with Mechthild Gawlick. *Martin Buber's "I and Thou": Practicing Living Dialogue*. Mahwah, NJ: Paulist Press, 2003.

Levinas, Emmanuel. "On Buber". In. *Levinas and Buber: Dialogue and Difference*, edited by Peter Atterton, Matthew Calarco, and Maurice Friedman, 32-36. Pittsburgh, PA: Duquesne University Press, 2004.

Lewisohn, Ludwig. *Rebirth, A Book of Modern Jewish Thought*. New York: Harper and Brothers, 1935.

Lutz, Mark A. "The Relevance of Martin Buber's Philosophical Anthropology for Economic Thought". In *Martin Buber and the Human Sciences*, edited by Maurice Friedman, 267–81. Albany, NY: State University of New York Press, 1996.

Mendes-Flohr, Paul. *From Mysticism to Dialogue: Martin Buber's Transformation of German Social Thought*. Detroit: Wayne State University Press, 1989.

ed. *Martin Buber: A Contemporary Perspective.* Syracuse: Syracuse University Press and Jerusalem: The Israel Academy of Sciences and Humanities, 2002.

"Buber's Rhetoric". In *Martin Buber: A Contemporary Perspective*, edited by Paul Mendes-Flohr, 1-24. Syracuse: Syracuse University Press and Jerusalem: The Israel Academy of Sciences and Humanities, 2002.

Moore, Donald J, SJ. "Martin Buber and Christian Theology: A Continuing Dialogue". In *Martin Buber and the Human Sciences*, edited by Maurice Friedman, 93-106. Albany, NY: State University of New York Press, 1996.

Nietzsche, Friedrich. "Beyond Good and Evil". In *Basic Writings of Nietzsche.* Translated and edited by Walter Kaufman. New York: Modern Library, 2000.

Ricoeur, Paul. *Freud and Philosophy: An Essay on Interpretation*. 2nd Edn. Translated by Denis Savage. New Haven: Yale University Press, 2002.

Rome, Sydney and Beatrice, eds. *Philosophical Interrogations*. New York: Harper Torchbooks, 1970.

Rose, Gillian. "Reply from 'The Single One': Soren Kierkegaard to Martin Buber".

In *Martin Buber: A Contemporary Perspective*, edited by Paul Mendes-Flohr, 148-165. Syracuse: Syracuse University Press and Jerusalem: The Israel Academy of Sciences and Humanities, 2002.

Rosenwald, Lawrence. "On the Reception of Buber and Rosenzweig's Bible". *Prooftexts* 14 (1994): 141-165.

Rotenstreich, Nathan. "The Right and the Limitations of Buber's Dialogical Thought". In *The Philosophy of Martin Buber*, eds. Paul Arthur Schilpp and Maurice Friedman, 97-132. LaSalle, IL: Open Court, 1967.

Schilpp, Paul Arthur, and Maurice Friedman, eds. *The Philosophy of Martin Buber*. LaSalle, IL: Open Court, 1967.

Shapira, Avraham. *Hope For Our Time: Key Trends In The Thought of Martin Buber*. Translated by Jeffrey M. Green. Albany, NY: State University of New York Press, 1999.

Wood, Robert E. *Martin Buber's Ontology: An Analysis of I and Thou*. Evanston: Northwestern University Press, 1969.

Zank, Michael. "Introduction". In *New Perspectives on Martin Buber*, edited by Michael Zank, 1–10. Tübingen: Mohr Siebeck, 2003.

THE MACAT LIBRARY
BY DISCIPLINE

AFRICANA STUDIES

Chinua Achebe's *An Image of Africa: Racism in Conrad's Heart of Darkness*
W. E. B. Du Bois's *The Souls of Black Folk*
Zora Neale Huston's *Characteristics of Negro Expression*
Martin Luther King Jr's *Why We Can't Wait*
Toni Morrison's *Playing in the Dark: Whiteness in the American Literary Imagination*

ANTHROPOLOGY

Arjun Appadurai's *Modernity at Large: Cultural Dimensions of Globalisation*
Philippe Ariès's *Centuries of Childhood*
Franz Boas's *Race, Language and Culture*
Kim Chan & Renée Mauborgne's *Blue Ocean Strategy*
Jared Diamond's *Guns, Germs & Steel: the Fate of Human Societies*
Jared Diamond's *Collapse: How Societies Choose to Fail or Survive*
E. E. Evans-Pritchard's *Witchcraft, Oracles and Magic Among the Azande*
James Ferguson's *The Anti-Politics Machine*
Clifford Geertz's *The Interpretation of Cultures*
David Graeber's *Debt: the First 5000 Years*
Karen Ho's *Liquidated: An Ethnography of Wall Street*
Geert Hofstede's *Culture's Consequences: Comparing Values, Behaviors, Institutes and Organizations across Nations*
Claude Lévi-Strauss's *Structural Anthropology*
Jay Macleod's *Ain't No Makin' It: Aspirations and Attainment in a Low-Income Neighborhood*
Saba Mahmood's *The Politics of Piety: The Islamic Revival and the Feminist Subjec*t
Marcel Mauss's *The Gift*

BUSINESS

Jean Lave & Etienne Wenger's *Situated Learning*
Theodore Levitt's *Marketing Myopia*
Burton G. Malkiel's *A Random Walk Down Wall Street*
Douglas McGregor's *The Human Side of Enterprise*
Michael Porter's *Competitive Strategy: Creating and Sustaining Superior Performance*
John Kotter's *Leading Change*
C. K. Prahalad & Gary Hamel's *The Core Competence of the Corporation*

CRIMINOLOGY

Michelle Alexander's *The New Jim Crow: Mass Incarceration in the Age of Colorblindness*
Michael R. Gottfredson & Travis Hirschi's *A General Theory of Crime*
Richard Herrnstein & Charles A. Murray's *The Bell Curve: Intelligence and Class Structure in American Life*
Elizabeth Loftus's *Eyewitness Testimony*
Jay Macleod's *Ain't No Makin' It: Aspirations and Attainment in a Low-Income Neighborhood*
Philip Zimbardo's *The Lucifer Effect*

ECONOMICS

Janet Abu-Lughod's *Before European Hegemony*
Ha-Joon Chang's *Kicking Away the Ladder*
David Brion Davis's *The Problem of Slavery in the Age of Revolution*
Milton Friedman's *The Role of Monetary Policy*
Milton Friedman's *Capitalism and Freedom*
David Graeber's *Debt: the First 5000 Years*
Friedrich Hayek's *The Road to Serfdom*
Karen Ho's *Liquidated: An Ethnography of Wall Street*

The Macat Library By Discipline

John Maynard Keynes's *The General Theory of Employment, Interest and Money*
Charles P. Kindleberger's *Manias, Panics and Crashes*
Robert Lucas's *Why Doesn't Capital Flow from Rich to Poor Countries?*
Burton G. Malkiel's *A Random Walk Down Wall Street*
Thomas Robert Malthus's *An Essay on the Principle of Population*
Karl Marx's *Capital*
Thomas Piketty's *Capital in the Twenty-First Century*
Amartya Sen's *Development as Freedom*
Adam Smith's *The Wealth of Nations*
Nassim Nicholas Taleb's *The Black Swan: The Impact of the Highly Improbable*
Amos Tversky's & Daniel Kahneman's *Judgment under Uncertainty: Heuristics and Biases*
Mahbub Ul Haq's *Reflections on Human Development*
Max Weber's *The Protestant Ethic and the Spirit of Capitalism*

FEMINISM AND GENDER STUDIES

Judith Butler's *Gender Trouble*
Simone De Beauvoir's *The Second Sex*
Michel Foucault's *History of Sexuality*
Betty Friedan's *The Feminine Mystique*
Saba Mahmood's *The Politics of Piety: The Islamic Revival and the Feminist Subject*
Joan Wallach Scott's *Gender and the Politics of History*
Mary Wollstonecraft's *A Vindication of the Rights of Woman*
Virginia Woolf's *A Room of One's Own*

GEOGRAPHY

The Brundtland Report's *Our Common Future*
Rachel Carson's *Silent Spring*
Charles Darwin's *On the Origin of Species*
James Ferguson's *The Anti-Politics Machine*
Jane Jacobs's *The Death and Life of Great American Cities*
James Lovelock's *Gaia: A New Look at Life on Earth*
Amartya Sen's *Development as Freedom*
Mathis Wackernagel & William Rees's *Our Ecological Footprint*

HISTORY

Janet Abu-Lughod's *Before European Hegemony*
Benedict Anderson's *Imagined Communities*
Bernard Bailyn's *The Ideological Origins of the American Revolution*
Hanna Batatu's *The Old Social Classes And The Revolutionary Movements Of Iraq*
Christopher Browning's *Ordinary Men: Reserve Police Batallion 101 and the Final Solution in Poland*
Edmund Burke's *Reflections on the Revolution in France*
William Cronon's *Nature's Metropolis: Chicago And The Great West*
Alfred W. Crosby's *The Columbian Exchange*
Hamid Dabashi's *Iran: A People Interrupted*
David Brion Davis's *The Problem of Slavery in the Age of Revolution*
Nathalie Zemon Davis's *The Return of Martin Guerre*
Jared Diamond's *Guns, Germs & Steel: the Fate of Human Societies*
Frank Dikotter's *Mao's Great Famine*
John W Dower's *War Without Mercy: Race And Power In The Pacific War*
W. E. B. Du Bois's *The Souls of Black Folk*
Richard J. Evans's *In Defence of History*
Lucien Febvre's *The Problem of Unbelief in the 16th Century*
Sheila Fitzpatrick's *Everyday Stalinism*

Eric Foner's *Reconstruction: America's Unfinished Revolution, 1863-1877*
Michel Foucault's *Discipline and Punish*
Michel Foucault's *History of Sexuality*
Francis Fukuyama's *The End of History and the Last Man*
John Lewis Gaddis's *We Now Know: Rethinking Cold War History*
Ernest Gellner's *Nations and Nationalism*
Eugene Genovese's *Roll, Jordan, Roll: The World the Slaves Made*
Carlo Ginzburg's *The Night Battles*
Daniel Goldhagen's *Hitler's Willing Executioners*
Jack Goldstone's *Revolution and Rebellion in the Early Modern World*
Antonio Gramsci's *The Prison Notebooks*
Alexander Hamilton, John Jay & James Madison's *The Federalist Papers*
Christopher Hill's *The World Turned Upside Down*
Carole Hillenbrand's *The Crusades: Islamic Perspectives*
Thomas Hobbes's *Leviathan*
Eric Hobsbawm's *The Age Of Revolution*
John A. Hobson's *Imperialism: A Study*
Albert Hourani's *History of the Arab Peoples*
Samuel P. Huntington's *The Clash of Civilizations and the Remaking of World Order*
C. L. R. James's *The Black Jacobins*
Tony Judt's *Postwar: A History of Europe Since 1945*
Ernst Kantorowicz's *The King's Two Bodies: A Study in Medieval Political Theology*
Paul Kennedy's *The Rise and Fall of the Great Powers*
Ian Kershaw's *The "Hitler Myth": Image and Reality in the Third Reich*
John Maynard Keynes's *The General Theory of Employment, Interest and Money*
Charles P. Kindleberger's *Manias, Panics and Crashes*
Martin Luther King Jr's *Why We Can't Wait*
Henry Kissinger's *World Order: Reflections on the Character of Nations and the Course of History*
Thomas Kuhn's *The Structure of Scientific Revolutions*
Georges Lefebvre's *The Coming of the French Revolution*
John Locke's *Two Treatises of Government*
Niccolò Machiavelli's *The Prince*
Thomas Robert Malthus's *An Essay on the Principle of Population*
Mahmood Mamdani's *Citizen and Subject: Contemporary Africa And The Legacy Of Late Colonialism*
Karl Marx's *Capital*
Stanley Milgram's *Obedience to Authority*
John Stuart Mill's *On Liberty*
Thomas Paine's *Common Sense*
Thomas Paine's *Rights of Man*
Geoffrey Parker's *Global Crisis: War, Climate Change and Catastrophe in the Seventeenth Century*
Jonathan Riley-Smith's *The First Crusade and the Idea of Crusading*
Jean-Jacques Rousseau's *The Social Contract*
Joan Wallach Scott's *Gender and the Politics of History*
Theda Skocpol's *States and Social Revolutions*
Adam Smith's *The Wealth of Nations*
Timothy Snyder's *Bloodlands: Europe Between Hitler and Stalin*
Sun Tzu's *The Art of War*
Keith Thomas's *Religion and the Decline of Magic*
Thucydides's *The History of the Peloponnesian War*
Frederick Jackson Turner's *The Significance of the Frontier in American History*
Odd Arne Westad's *The Global Cold War: Third World Interventions And The Making Of Our Times*

The Macat Library By Discipline

LITERATURE

Chinua Achebe's *An Image of Africa: Racism in Conrad's Heart of Darkness*
Roland Barthes's *Mythologies*
Homi K. Bhabha's *The Location of Culture*
Judith Butler's *Gender Trouble*
Simone De Beauvoir's *The Second Sex*
Ferdinand De Saussure's *Course in General Linguistics*
T. S. Eliot's *The Sacred Wood: Essays on Poetry and Criticism*
Zora Neale Huston's *Characteristics of Negro Expression*
Toni Morrison's *Playing in the Dark: Whiteness in the American Literary Imagination*
Edward Said's *Orientalism*
Gayatri Chakravorty Spivak's *Can the Subaltern Speak?*
Mary Wollstonecraft's *A Vindication of the Rights of Women*
Virginia Woolf's *A Room of One's Own*

PHILOSOPHY

Elizabeth Anscombe's *Modern Moral Philosophy*
Hannah Arendt's *The Human Condition*
Aristotle's *Metaphysics*
Aristotle's *Nicomachean Ethics*
Edmund Gettier's *Is Justified True Belief Knowledge?*
Georg Wilhelm Friedrich Hegel's *Phenomenology of Spirit*
David Hume's *Dialogues Concerning Natural Religion*
David Hume's *The Enquiry for Human Understanding*
Immanuel Kant's *Religion within the Boundaries of Mere Reason*
Immanuel Kant's *Critique of Pure Reason*
Søren Kierkegaard's *The Sickness Unto Death*
Søren Kierkegaard's *Fear and Trembling*
C. S. Lewis's *The Abolition of Man*
Alasdair MacIntyre's *After Virtue*
Marcus Aurelius's *Meditations*
Friedrich Nietzsche's *On the Genealogy of Morality*
Friedrich Nietzsche's *Beyond Good and Evil*
Plato's *Republic*
Plato's *Symposium*
Jean-Jacques Rousseau's *The Social Contract*
Gilbert Ryle's *The Concept of Mind*
Baruch Spinoza's *Ethics*
Sun Tzu's *The Art of War*
Ludwig Wittgenstein's *Philosophical Investigations*

POLITICS

Benedict Anderson's *Imagined Communities*
Aristotle's *Politics*
Bernard Bailyn's *The Ideological Origins of the American Revolution*
Edmund Burke's *Reflections on the Revolution in France*
John C. Calhoun's *A Disquisition on Government*
Ha-Joon Chang's *Kicking Away the Ladder*
Hamid Dabashi's *Iran: A People Interrupted*
Hamid Dabashi's *Theology of Discontent: The Ideological Foundation of the Islamic Revolution in Iran*
Robert Dahl's *Democracy and its Critics*
Robert Dahl's *Who Governs?*
David Brion Davis's *The Problem of Slavery in the Age of Revolution*

Alexis De Tocqueville's *Democracy in America*
James Ferguson's *The Anti-Politics Machine*
Frank Dikotter's *Mao's Great Famine*
Sheila Fitzpatrick's *Everyday Stalinism*
Eric Foner's *Reconstruction: America's Unfinished Revolution, 1863-1877*
Milton Friedman's *Capitalism and Freedom*
Francis Fukuyama's *The End of History and the Last Man*
John Lewis Gaddis's *We Now Know: Rethinking Cold War History*
Ernest Gellner's *Nations and Nationalism*
David Graeber's *Debt: the First 5000 Years*
Antonio Gramsci's *The Prison Notebooks*
Alexander Hamilton, John Jay & James Madison's *The Federalist Papers*
Friedrich Hayek's *The Road to Serfdom*
Christopher Hill's *The World Turned Upside Down*
Thomas Hobbes's *Leviathan*
John A. Hobson's *Imperialism: A Study*
Samuel P. Huntington's *The Clash of Civilizations and the Remaking of World Order*
Tony Judt's *Postwar: A History of Europe Since 1945*
David C. Kang's *China Rising: Peace, Power and Order in East Asia*
Paul Kennedy's *The Rise and Fall of Great Powers*
Robert Keohane's *After Hegemony*
Martin Luther King Jr.'s *Why We Can't Wait*
Henry Kissinger's *World Order: Reflections on the Character of Nations and the Course of History*
John Locke's *Two Treatises of Government*
Niccolò Machiavelli's *The Prince*
Thomas Robert Malthus's *An Essay on the Principle of Population*
Mahmood Mamdani's *Citizen and Subject: Contemporary Africa And The Legacy Of Late Colonialism*
Karl Marx's *Capital*
John Stuart Mill's *On Liberty*
John Stuart Mill's *Utilitarianism*
Hans Morgenthau's *Politics Among Nations*
Thomas Paine's *Common Sense*
Thomas Paine's *Rights of Man*
Thomas Piketty's *Capital in the Twenty-First Century*
Robert D. Putnam's *Bowling Alone*
John Rawls's *Theory of Justice*
Jean-Jacques Rousseau's *The Social Contract*
Theda Skocpol's *States and Social Revolutions*
Adam Smith's *The Wealth of Nations*
Sun Tzu's *The Art of War*
Henry David Thoreau's *Civil Disobedience*
Thucydides's *The History of the Peloponnesian War*
Kenneth Waltz's *Theory of International Politics*
Max Weber's *Politics as a Vocation*
Odd Arne Westad's *The Global Cold War: Third World Interventions And The Making Of Our Times*

POSTCOLONIAL STUDIES

Roland Barthes's *Mythologies*
Frantz Fanon's *Black Skin, White Masks*
Homi K. Bhabha's *The Location of Culture*
Gustavo Gutiérrez's *A Theology of Liberation*
Edward Said's *Orientalism*
Gayatri Chakravorty Spivak's *Can the Subaltern Speak?*

PSYCHOLOGY

Gordon Allport's *The Nature of Prejudice*
Alan Baddeley & Graham Hitch's *Aggression: A Social Learning Analysis*
Albert Bandura's *Aggression: A Social Learning Analysis*
Leon Festinger's *A Theory of Cognitive Dissonance*
Sigmund Freud's *The Interpretation of Dreams*
Betty Friedan's *The Feminine Mystique*
Michael R. Gottfredson & Travis Hirschi's *A General Theory of Crime*
Eric Hoffer's *The True Believer: Thoughts on the Nature of Mass Movements*
William James's *Principles of Psychology*
Elizabeth Loftus's *Eyewitness Testimony*
A. H. Maslow's *A Theory of Human Motivation*
Stanley Milgram's *Obedience to Authority*
Steven Pinker's *The Better Angels of Our Nature*
Oliver Sacks's *The Man Who Mistook His Wife For a Hat*
Richard Thaler & Cass Sunstein's *Nudge: Improving Decisions About Health, Wealth and Happiness*
Amos Tversky's *Judgment under Uncertainty: Heuristics and Biases*
Philip Zimbardo's *The Lucifer Effect*

SCIENCE

Rachel Carson's *Silent Spring*
William Cronon's *Nature's Metropolis: Chicago And The Great West*
Alfred W. Crosby's *The Columbian Exchange*
Charles Darwin's *On the Origin of Species*
Richard Dawkin's *The Selfish Gene*
Thomas Kuhn's *The Structure of Scientific Revolutions*
Geoffrey Parker's *Global Crisis: War, Climate Change and Catastrophe in the Seventeenth Century*
Mathis Wackernagel & William Rees's *Our Ecological Footprint*

SOCIOLOGY

Michelle Alexander's *The New Jim Crow: Mass Incarceration in the Age of Colorblindness*
Gordon Allport's *The Nature of Prejudice*
Albert Bandura's *Aggression: A Social Learning Analysis*
Hanna Batatu's *The Old Social Classes And The Revolutionary Movements Of Iraq*
Ha-Joon Chang's *Kicking Away the Ladder*
W. E. B. Du Bois's *The Souls of Black Folk*
Émile Durkheim's *On Suicide*
Frantz Fanon's *Black Skin, White Masks*
Frantz Fanon's *The Wretched of the Earth*
Eric Foner's *Reconstruction: America's Unfinished Revolution, 1863-1877*
Eugene Genovese's *Roll, Jordan, Roll: The World the Slaves Made*
Jack Goldstone's *Revolution and Rebellion in the Early Modern World*
Antonio Gramsci's *The Prison Notebooks*
Richard Herrnstein & Charles A Murray's *The Bell Curve: Intelligence and Class Structure in American Life*
Eric Hoffer's *The True Believer: Thoughts on the Nature of Mass Movements*
Jane Jacobs's *The Death and Life of Great American Cities*
Robert Lucas's *Why Doesn't Capital Flow from Rich to Poor Countries?*
Jay Macleod's *Ain't No Makin' It: Aspirations and Attainment in a Low Income Neighborhood*
Elaine May's *Homeward Bound: American Families in the Cold War Era*
Douglas McGregor's *The Human Side of Enterprise*
C. Wright Mills's *The Sociological Imagination*

Thomas Piketty's *Capital in the Twenty-First Century*
Robert D. Putman's *Bowling Alone*
David Riesman's *The Lonely Crowd: A Study of the Changing American Character*
Edward Said's *Orientalism*
Joan Wallach Scott's *Gender and the Politics of History*
Theda Skocpol's *States and Social Revolutions*
Max Weber's *The Protestant Ethic and the Spirit of Capitalism*

THEOLOGY

Augustine's *Confessions*
Benedict's *Rule of St Benedict*
Gustavo Gutiérrez's *A Theology of Liberation*
Carole Hillenbrand's *The Crusades: Islamic Perspectives*
David Hume's *Dialogues Concerning Natural Religion*
Immanuel Kant's *Religion within the Boundaries of Mere Reason*
Ernst Kantorowicz's *The King's Two Bodies: A Study in Medieval Political Theology*
Søren Kierkegaard's *The Sickness Unto Death*
C. S. Lewis's *The Abolition of Man*
Saba Mahmood's *The Politics of Piety: The Islamic Revival and the Feminist Subject*
Baruch Spinoza's *Ethics*
Keith Thomas's *Religion and the Decline of Magic*

Macat Disciplines

Access the greatest ideas and thinkers across entire disciplines, including

AFRICANA STUDIES

Chinua Achebe's *An Image of Africa: Racism in Conrad's Heart of Darkness*

W. E. B. Du Bois's *The Souls of Black Folk*

Zora Neale Hurston's *Characteristics of Negro Expression*

Martin Luther King Jr.'s *Why We Can't Wait*

Toni Morrison's *Playing in the Dark: Whiteness in the American Literary Imagination*

Macat analyses are available from all good bookshops and libraries.

Access hundreds of analyses through one, multimedia tool.
Join free for one month **library.macat.com**

Macat Disciplines

Access the greatest ideas and thinkers across entire disciplines, including

FEMINISM, GENDER AND QUEER STUDIES

Simone De Beauvoir's
The Second Sex

Michel Foucault's
History of Sexuality

Betty Friedan's
The Feminine Mystique

Saba Mahmood's
*The Politics of Piety:
The Islamic Revival and
the Feminist Subject*

Joan Wallach Scott's
*Gender and the
Politics of History*

Mary Wollstonecraft's
*A Vindication of the
Rights of Woman*

Virginia Woolf's
A Room of One's Own

Judith Butler's
Gender Trouble

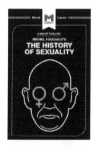

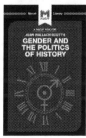

Macat analyses are available from all good bookshops and libraries.

Access hundreds of analyses through one, multimedia tool.
Join free for one month **library.macat.com**

Macat Disciplines

Access the greatest ideas and thinkers across entire disciplines, including

INEQUALITY

Ha-Joon Chang's, *Kicking Away the Ladder*

David Graeber's, *Debt: The First 5000 Years*

Robert E. Lucas's, *Why Doesn't Capital Flow from Rich To Poor Countries?*

Thomas Piketty's, *Capital in the Twenty-First Century*

Amartya Sen's, *Inequality Re-Examined*

Mahbub Ul Haq's, *Reflections on Human Development*

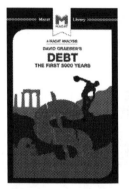
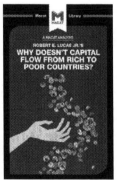

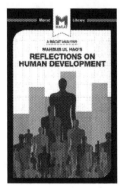

Macat analyses are available from all good bookshops and libraries.

Access hundreds of analyses through one, multimedia tool.

Join free for one month **library.macat.com**

Macat Disciplines

Access the greatest ideas and thinkers across entire disciplines, including

CRIMINOLOGY

Michelle Alexander's
The New Jim Crow: Mass Incarceration in the Age of Colorblindness

Michael R. Gottfredson & Travis Hirschi's
A General Theory of Crime

Elizabeth Loftus's
Eyewitness Testimony

Richard Herrnstein & Charles A. Murray's
The Bell Curve: Intelligence and Class Structure in American Life

Jay Macleod's
Ain't No Makin' It: Aspirations and Attainment in a Low-Income Neighborhood

Philip Zimbardo's
The Lucifer Effect

Macat Disciplines

Access the greatest ideas and thinkers across entire disciplines, including

Postcolonial Studies

Roland Barthes's *Mythologies*
Frantz Fanon's *Black Skin, White Masks*
Homi K. Bhabha's *The Location of Culture*
Gustavo Gutiérrez's *A Theology of Liberation*
Edward Said's *Orientalism*
Gayatri Chakravorty Spivak's *Can the Subaltern Speak?*

Macat analyses are available from all good bookshops and libraries.

Access hundreds of analyses through one, multimedia tool.
Join free for one month **library.macat.com**

Macat Disciplines

Access the greatest ideas and thinkers across entire disciplines, including

GLOBALIZATION

Arjun Appadurai's, *Modernity at Large: Cultural Dimensions of Globalisation*

James Ferguson's, *The Anti-Politics Machine*

Geert Hofstede's, *Culture's Consequences*

Amartya Sen's, *Development as Freedom*

Macat Pairs

Analyse historical and modern issues from opposite sides of an argument.
Pairs include:

HOW TO RUN AN ECONOMY

John Maynard Keynes's
The General Theory OF Employment, Interest and Money

Classical economics suggests that market economies are self-correcting in times of recession or depression, and tend toward full employment and output. But English economist John Maynard Keynes disagrees.

In his ground-breaking 1936 study *The General Theory*, Keynes argues that traditional economics has misunderstood the causes of unemployment. Employment is not determined by the price of labor; it is directly linked to demand. Keynes believes market economies are by nature unstable, and so require government intervention. Spurred on by the social catastrophe of the Great Depression of the 1930s, he sets out to revolutionize the way the world thinks

Milton Friedman's
The Role of Monetary Policy

Friedman's 1968 paper changed the course of economic theory. In just 17 pages, he demolished existing theory and outlined an effective alternate monetary policy designed to secure 'high employment, stable prices and rapid growth.'

Friedman demonstrated that monetary policy plays a vital role in broader economic stability and argued that economists got their monetary policy wrong in the 1950s and 1960s by misunderstanding the relationship between inflation and unemployment. Previous generations of economists had believed that governments could permanently decrease unemployment by permitting inflation—and vice versa. Friedman's most original contribution was to show that this supposed trade-off is an illusion that only works in the short term.

Macat analyses are available from all good bookshops and libraries.

Access hundreds of analyses through one, multimedia tool.
Join free for one month **library.macat.com**

Macat Disciplines

Access the greatest ideas and thinkers across entire disciplines, including

THE FUTURE OF DEMOCRACY

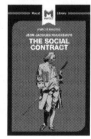

Robert A. Dahl's, *Democracy and Its Critics*
Robert A. Dahl's, *Who Governs?*
Alexis De Toqueville's, *Democracy in America*
Niccolò Machiavelli's, *The Prince*
John Stuart Mill's, *On Liberty*
Robert D. Putnam's, *Bowling Alone*
Jean-Jacques Rousseau's, *The Social Contract*
Henry David Thoreau's, *Civil Disobedience*

Macat Disciplines

Access the greatest ideas and thinkers across entire disciplines, including

TOTALITARIANISM

Sheila Fitzpatrick's, *Everyday Stalinism*
Ian Kershaw's, *The "Hitler Myth"*
Timothy Snyder's, *Bloodlands*

Macat Pairs

*Analyse historical and modern issues from opposite sides of an argument.
Pairs include:*

RACE AND IDENTITY

Zora Neale Hurston's
Characteristics of Negro Expression

Using material collected on anthropological expeditions to the South, Zora Neale Hurston explains how expression in African American culture in the early twentieth century departs from the art of white America. At the time, African American art was often criticized for copying white culture. For Hurston, this criticism misunderstood how art works. European tradition views art as something fixed. But Hurston describes a creative process that is alive, ever-changing, and largely improvisational. She maintains that African American art works through a process called 'mimicry'—where an imitated object or verbal pattern, for example, is reshaped and altered until it becomes something new, novel—and worthy of attention.

Frantz Fanon's
Black Skin, White Masks

Black Skin, White Masks offers a radical analysis of the psychological effects of colonization on the colonized.

Fanon witnessed the effects of colonization first hand both in his birthplace, Martinique, and again later in life when he worked as a psychiatrist in another French colony, Algeria. His text is uncompromising in form and argument. He dissects the dehumanizing effects of colonialism, arguing that it destroys the native sense of identity, forcing people to adapt to an alien set of values—including a core belief that they are inferior. This results in deep psychological trauma.

Fanon's work played a pivotal role in the civil rights movements of the 1960s.

Macat analyses are available from all good bookshops and libraries.

Access hundreds of analyses through one, multimedia tool.
Join free for one month **library.macat.com**

Macat Pairs

Analyse historical and modern issues from opposite sides of an argument. Pairs include:

INTERNATIONAL RELATIONS IN THE 21ST CENTURY

Samuel P. Huntington's
The Clash of Civilisations

In his highly influential 1996 book, Huntington offers a vision of a post-Cold War world in which conflict takes place not between competing ideologies but between cultures. The worst clash, he argues, will be between the Islamic world and the West: the West's arrogance and belief that its culture is a "gift" to the world will come into conflict with Islam's obstinacy and concern that its culture is under attack from a morally decadent "other."

Clash inspired much debate between different political schools of thought. But its greatest impact came in helping define American foreign policy in the wake of the 2001 terrorist attacks in New York and Washington.

Francis Fukuyama's
The End of History and the Last Man

Published in 1992, *The End of History and the Last Man* argues that capitalist democracy is the final destination for all societies. Fukuyama believed democracy triumphed during the Cold War because it lacks the "fundamental contradictions" inherent in communism and satisfies our yearning for freedom and equality. Democracy therefore marks the endpoint in the evolution of ideology, and so the "end of history." There will still be "events," but no fundamental change in ideology.

Macat Disciplines

Access the greatest ideas and thinkers across entire disciplines, including

MAN AND THE ENVIRONMENT

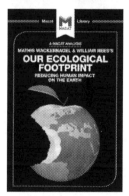

The Brundtland Report's, *Our Common Future*
Rachel Carson's, *Silent Spring*
James Lovelock's, *Gaia: A New Look at Life on Earth*
Mathis Wackernagel & William Rees's, *Our Ecological Footprint*

Macat Pairs

Analyse historical and modern issues from opposite sides of an argument. Pairs include:

Steven Pinker's
The Better Angels of Our Nature

Stephen Pinker's gloriously optimistic 2011 book argues that, despite humanity's biological tendency toward violence, we are, in fact, less violent today than ever before. To prove his case, Pinker lays out pages of detailed statistical evidence. For him, much of the credit for the decline goes to the eighteenth-century Enlightenment movement, whose ideas of liberty, tolerance, and respect for the value of human life filtered down through society and affected how people thought. That psychological change led to behavioral change—and overall we became more peaceful. Critics countered that humanity could never overcome the biological urge toward violence; others argued that Pinker's statistics were flawed.

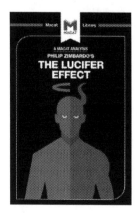

Philip Zimbardo's
The Lucifer Effect

Some psychologists believe those who commit cruelty are innately evil. Zimbardo disagrees. In *The Lucifer Effect*, he argues that sometimes good people do evil things simply because of the situations they find themselves in, citing many historical examples to illustrate his point. Zimbardo details his 1971 Stanford prison experiment, where ordinary volunteers playing guards in a mock prison rapidly became abusive. But he also describes the tortures committed by US army personnel in Iraq's Abu Ghraib prison in 2003—and how he himself testified in defence of one of those guards. committed by US army personnel in Iraq's Abu Ghraib prison in 2003—and how he himself testified in defence of one of those guards.

Macat Pairs

Analyse historical and modern issues from opposite sides of an argument. Pairs include:

HOW WE RELATE TO EACH OTHER AND SOCIETY

Jean-Jacques Rousseau's
The Social Contract

Rousseau's famous work sets out the radical concept of the 'social contract': a give-and-take relationship between individual freedom and social order.

If people are free to do as they like, governed only by their own sense of justice, they are also vulnerable to chaos and violence. To avoid this, Rousseau proposes, they should agree to give up some freedom to benefit from the protection of social and political organization. But this deal is only just if societies are led by the collective needs and desires of the people, and able to control the private interests of individuals. For Rousseau, the only legitimate form of government is rule by the people.

Robert D. Putnam's
Bowling Alone

In *Bowling Alone*, Robert Putnam argues that Americans have become disconnected from one another and from the institutions of their common life, and investigates the consequences of this change.

Looking at a range of indicators, from membership in formal organizations to the number of invitations being extended to informal dinner parties, Putnam demonstrates that Americans are interacting less and creating less "social capital" – with potentially disastrous implications for their society.

It would be difficult to overstate the impact of *Bowling Alone*, one of the most frequently cited social science publications of the last half-century.

Macat analyses are available from all good bookshops and libraries.

Access hundreds of analyses through one, multimedia tool.
Join free for one month **library.macat.com**

Printed in the United States
by Baker & Taylor Publisher Services